Human Rights Record of the United States in 2015

2015年美国的人权纪录

State Council Information Office of the People's Republic of China

中华人民共和国国务院新闻办公室

图书在版编目（CIP）数据

2015年美国的人权纪录：汉英对照 / 中华人民共和国国务院新闻办公室编. -- 北京：五洲传播出版社, 2016.4
ISBN 978-7-5085-3363-6

Ⅰ. ①2… Ⅱ. ①中… Ⅲ. ①人权－白皮书－美国－2015－汉、英 Ⅳ. ①D771.224

中国版本图书馆CIP数据核字(2016)第058213号

2015年美国的人权纪录

责任编辑　高　磊
制　　作　张　红
出版发行　五洲传播出版社
地　　址　北京市海淀区北三环中路31号生产力大楼B座6层
邮政编码　100088
电　　话　010－82005927　82007837（发行部）
网　　址　http://www.cicc.org.cn
印　　刷　北京光之彩印刷有限公司
开　　本　889mm*1194mm　1/32
印　　张　3.5
字　　数　50千
版　　次　2016年4月第1版
印　　次　2016年4月第1次印刷
定　　价　32.00元

Contents
目　录

Human Rights Record of the United States in 2015

State Council Information Office of the People's Republic of China

April 2016

Foreword

On April 13 local time, the State Department of the United States released its country reports on human rights practices. It made comments on the human rights situation in many countries once again while being tight-lipped about its own terrible human rights record and showing not a bit of intention to reflect on it. In 2015, the United States saw no improvement in its existent human rights issues, but reported numerous new problems. Since the U.S. government refuses to hold up a mirror to look at itself, it has to be done with other people's help.

The following facts about the U.S. human rights situation in 2015 are supported by irrefutable records.

– The use of guns was out of control in the United States, which severely threatened citizens' right of life. The frequent occurrence of shooting incidents was the deepest impression left to the world concerning the United States in 2015. There were a total of 51,675 gun violence incidents in the United States in 2015 as of December 28, leaving 13,136 killed and 26,493 injured.

– Citizens' personal security could not be guaranteed with the excessive use of violence by police. Police shot dead 965 people last year as of December 24, and the abuse of power by the police did not result in discipline. "Justice for Freddie" protests were staged in Baltimore, demonstrators in Chicago took to the street to demand justice in the death of Laquan MacDonald, and protesters in Minneapolis camped outside a police precinct after Jamar Clark was shot dead by police.

– The prison system in the United States was plagued by corruption and severely violated inmates' human rights. The guards in a prison in Florida scalded a mentally-ill inmate Darren Rainey to death in hot shower. The guards in Lowell Correctional Institution, the nation's largest women's prison, pressured hundreds of female inmates to barter sex for basic necessities and a shield from abuse, and 57 inmates have died in this prison over the past 10 years.

– Money politics and clan politics were prevailing and the political rights of the citizens were not safeguarded effectively. Companies and individuals were able to donate an unlimited size to super Political Action Committees (super PACs) to influence the presidential election. In this way, corporations could use money to sway politics and reap tremendous returns. There were comments that the political system of the United States had been subverted to be a tool that provided returns to major political donors. Family pedigree had become a primary factor for U.S. politics, with a few families and behind-the-scenes interest groups influencing the election using funds. The popular will was abducted by factionalism in the United States, because the interests involved in election made it unable for the Democratic Party and the Republican Party to coordinate on and work out policies that were in line with the popular will.

– The lingering problems in U.S. society posed challenges for the country to fulfill its duty of safeguarding the economic and social rights of U.S. citizens. In 2014, there were 46.7 million people in poverty in the United States. Every year, at least 48.1 million people were classed as "food insecure." In 2015, more than 560,000 people nationwide were homeless. Seventy-nine percent of Americans believed it was more common for people to fall out of the middle class than rise up to it. There were still 33 million people in the United States with no healthcare insurance, and 44 million private-sector workers, about 40 percent of the total, did not have access to paid sick leaves.

– Racial conflict was severe in the United States, with race relations at their worst in nearly two decades. Sixty-one percent of Americans characterized race relations in the United States as "bad." Law enforcement and justice fields were heavily affected by racial discrimination, with 88 percent of African-Americans believing they were treated unfairly by police, and 68 percent of African-Americans believing the American criminal justice system was racially biased. Whites had 12 times the wealth of blacks and nearly 10 times more than Hispanics. It was said that the American Dream remained out of reach for many African-American and Hispanic families.

– The situation for American women was deteriorating and children were living in worrisome environment. In 2014, women in the United States were paid 79 cents for every dollar paid to men. The percentage of women in poverty increased from 12.1 percent to 14.5 percent over the past decade. The United Nations' International Labor Organization said that the United States was the only industrialized nation with no overall law for cash benefits provided to women during maternity leave. A total of 23 percent of undergraduate women said they were victims of non-consensual sexual contact. There were at least two school shootings a month in 2015 and almost two children were killed every week in unintentional shootings. About a quarter of the teenagers above 15 years old who died of injuries in the United States were killed in gun-related incidents. About 17.4 million children under the age of 18 were being raised without a father and 45 percent lived below the poverty line. About one fifth of all U.S. children lived in food-insecure households.

– The United States still brazenly and brutally violated human rights in other countries, treating citizens from other countries like dirt. Air strikes launched by the United States in Iraq and Syria killed thousands of civilians. The United States also conducted drone attacks in Pakistan and Yemen indiscriminately, causing hundreds of civilian deaths. On October 3, 2015, the U.S. military bombed a hospital operated by "Doctors Without Borders" in the city of Kunduz in Afghanistan, in which 42 people were killed. Defying international condemnation, the United States still did not close the Guantanamo Bay detention camp, which had been running for 14 years and still locked up nearly 100 people who had been under arbitrary detention for years without trial.

I. Wanton Infringement on Civil Rights

Civil rights were wantonly infringed upon in the United States in 2015 with rampant gun-related crimes, excessive use of force by police, severe corruption in prisons and frequent occurrence of illegal eavesdropping on personal information.

Citizen's life and property security were threatened by violent crimes. According to the report "Crime in the United States" released by the FBI in 2015, an estimated 1,165,383 violent crimes occurred nationwide in 2014, of which 14,249 were murders, 84,041 were rapes, 325,802 robberies and 741,291 aggravated assaults. Nationwide, there were an estimated 8,277,829 property crimes, with the victims of such crimes suffering losses calculated at an estimated 14.3 billion U.S. dollars. The statistics showed the estimated rate of violent crime was 365.5 offenses per 100,000 inhabitants, and the property crime rate was 2,596.1 offenses per 100,000 inhabitants (www.fbi.gov). Many cities in the United States saw large jumps in crime during the first half of 2015: the murder rate rose 48 percent and 59 percent compared to the same period of the previous year in Baltimore and St. Louis, respectively, said an article carried by *the Economist* website on December 1, 2015 (www.economist.com, December

1, 2015). James Howell of the U.S. National Gang Center pointed out that in the past five years the United States had seen an 8 percent increase in the number of gangs, an 11 percent increase in members and a 23 percent increase in gang-related homicides (www.usnews.com, March 6, 2015).

Citizen's right of life could not be guaranteed with the rampant use of guns. Statistics showed that there were more than 300 million guns in the United States which had a population of more than 300 million. Over the past decade, more than 4 million U.S. citizens became victims of assaults, robberies and other gun-related crimes. According to a toll report by the Gun Violence Archive, there were a total of 51,675 gun violence incidents in the United States last year as of December 28, including 329 mass shootings. Altogether 13,136 were killed and 26,493 injured (www.gunviolencearchive.org, December 28, 2015). According to the report "Crime in the United States" released by the FBI in 2015, firearms were used in 67.9 percent of the nation's murders, 40.3 percent of robberies, and 22.5 percent of aggravated assaults in 2014 (www.fbi.gov).

Excessive use of violence by police gravely violated human rights. Excessive use of violence by police during law enforcement had resulted in a large number of civilian casualties. Police shot dead 965 people last year as of December 24, according to data posted on *The Washington Post* website (www.washingtonpost.com, December 24, 2015). Freddie Gray, a 25-year-old African-American man, died while in police custody in Baltimore. His death, reportedly a result of violence by the police, sparked

"Justice for Freddie" protests (www.usatoday.com, December 22, 2015). Outraged that it took too long to charge a Chicago police officer in African-American Laquan MacDonald's shooting death, demonstrators took to the street to demand justice in his death. The police officer had a history of 20 complaints before he gunned down the 17-year-old, but none resulted in discipline (edition.cnn.com, November 26, 2015). According to a report by the NBC News on November 19, 2015, protestors camped outside a police precinct in Minneapolis after African-American Jamar Clark, 24, was shot dead when he was already under police control. The demonstrations turned violent later (www.nbc.com, November 19, 2015).

The government infringed on citizens' privacy by illegally eavesdropping personal information. According to a report carried by the website of *The Washington Post* on December 1, 2015, the FBI used special authority to compel Internet firms to hand over user information, including full browsing histories, without court approvals (www.washingtonpost.com, December 1, 2015). According to a report released by the Pew Research Center on May 29, 2015, a majority of Americans opposed the government collecting bulk data on its citizens, two-thirds believed there weren't adequate limits on what types of data could be collected, 61 percent said they had become less confident that the programs were serving the public interests, 54 percent of Americans disapproved of the U.S. government's collection of telephone and Internet data as part of anti-terrorism efforts, and 74 percent said they should not give up privacy and freedom for the sake of safety. Most said it was important to control who could get their information (93 percent), as well as what information about them was collected (90 percent) (www.pewresearch.org, May 29, 2015).

Prison guards wantonly trampled on prisoners' human rights. According to a serial report on the website of *the Miami Herald* in December 2015, Lowell Correctional Institution, the nation's largest women's prison, was haunted by corruption, torment and sex abuse. The guards took hundreds of female inmates as whores and pressured them to barter sex for basic necessities, a shield from abuse or awards. In the past 10 years 57 inmates died in the prison, not accounting those who make it to hospital (www.miamiherald.com, December 12, 13 and 16, 2015). *The Washington Post* reported on its website on May 13, 2015 that a guard in the Fairfax County jail killed a mentally ill woman, Natasha McKenna, with a Taser stun gun (www.washingtonpost.com, May 13, 2015). The Fox News reported on its website on April 9, 2015 that guards in a prison in Florida was accused of abusing and even killing inmates. In one case, a mentally-ill inmate Darren Rainey was forced to take a shower for two hours with the water reportedly rigged to a scalding 180 degrees Fahrenheit. Despite his calls for help, no one came. He reportedly died after his skin was partially burned off his body (www.foxnews.com, April 9, 2015).

II. Political Rights Not Safeguarded

In 2015, money politics and clan politics went from bad to

worse in the nation where voters found it hard to express their real volition and there was discrimination against belief in political life. In addition, citizens' right to information was further suppressed. Unsurprisingly, former U.S. President Jimmy Carter said that "the U.S. is no longer a democracy" (www.huffingtonpost.com, August 3, 2015).

Money politics revealed the hypocrisy in democracy. Although the laws of the United States put a lid on the size of individual donations to presidential candidates, there is no limit for such contributions to super PACs by individuals and corporations. *The USA Today* reported on April 10, 2015 that the allies of at least 11 White House hopefuls had launched committees to raise unlimited money to back their campaigns (www.usatoday.com, April 10, 2015). The presidential candidates and the super PACs raised about 380 million U.S. dollars in only half a year. More than 60 donations were worth more than 1 million U.S. dollars each, accounting for about one third of the total contributions. Half of the amount came from those who donated more than 100,000 U.S. dollars and the combined fund of the top 67 donors was more than three times that of 508,000 donors with least contributions (www.aol.com, August 1; www.politico.com, August 1). According to a report of the Zerohedge, between 2007 and 2012, 200 of America's most politically active corporations spent a combined 5.8 billion U.S. dollars on federal lobbying and campaign contributions. What they gave paled compared to what those same corporations got: 4.4 trillion U.S. dollars in federal business and support. Put that in context, the sum represented two thirds of what individual taxpayers paid into the federal treasury. For every dollar spent on influencing politics, the nation's most politically active corporations received 760 U.S. dollars from the government (www.zerohedge.com, March 16, 2015). Jimmy Carter said that with unlimited political bribery being the essence of getting the nominations for president or being elected president, the U.S. political system was subverted to be a payoff to major contributors (www.huffingtonpost.com, August 3, 2015). The role money played in politics was also indicated in the U.S. President's State of the Union Address for 2016, which said a handful of families and hidden interests were exercising influence on elections via their funds.

Clan politics was driving U.S. government elections. Among the candidates for the 2016 presidential election, more than one candidate was obviously related to clan politics. *The New York Times* concluded through big data analysis that advantages from father generation played a role in politics obviously. The chance for the son of a U.S. president to become president was 1.4 million times higher than his peers. Meanwhile the chance for a governor's son to be elected governor was 6,000 times higher than ordinary people. In addition, the chance for the son of a senator to be a senator like his father was also 8,500 times higher than ordinary U.S. men (www.nytimes.com, March 22, 2015). *The Washington Post* reported on January 16, 2015 that since the beginning of the Republic, 8.7 percent of its members of Congress were closely related to someone who had served in the body. The report continued to point out that a smell of heirship could be detected in the U.S. presidential election since the possible slate of candidates would include the son of a governor and presidential candidate, the son of a congressman and presidential candidate, the wife of a president and the brother of a president, son of a president and grandson of a senator (www.washingtonpost.com, January 16, 2015).

Discrimination against beliefs led to unfairness in political life. Not believing in God could be the biggest disadvantage while running for a post in public office. It was difficult for those who were not Christians to win elections and for those who did not have a religious belief, the chance to win elections was slimmer. In a May 2014 Pew Research survey, atheism was the most disqualifying factor for a potential presidential candidate, according to a report posted on the website of *The Washington Post* on September 22, 2015. More than half of those surveyed said they would be less likely to vote for someone who did not believe in God. And another Pew poll in July 2014 found that of all religion-related groups, atheists and Muslims were viewed the most negatively by Americans (www.washingtonpost.com, September 22, 2015).

Citizens' electoral rights were further limited. According to an article on the website of *the U.S. News and World Report* on August 4, 2015, since 2010, a total of 21 states had adopted new laws to limit the exercise of suffrage. Some states shortened the time for early voting, while others limited the number of documents identifying one as a lawful voter. A total of 14 states will carry out fresh measures to limit the exercise of suffrage for the first time in 2016 presidential election. The voting rights were hit by the vicious competition between the two parties. One Democratic candidate accused GOP presidential candidates of having "systematically and deliberately" tried to keep millions of Americans from voting so as to win the election (www.usnews.com, August 4, 2015). A *USA Today* report, which was published on its website on March 20, 2015, said the nation had its lowest midterm-election voter turnout in 2014 since the early 1940s. The average turnout across the United States was 37 percent, with a low of 28.8 percent recorded in Indiana (www.usatoday.com, March 20, 2015).

It was difficult for voters to express their real will. *The Christian Science Monitor* carried a report on its website on December 13, 2015 that the two-party system forced the voters to take side. Most voters cast ballots for a party not because they supported the party but out of fear and worry over the other one (www.csmonitor.com, December 13, 2015). It was said in the U.S. President's State of the Union Address for 2016 that the practice of drawing congressional districts led to the situation where "politicians can pick their voters, and not the other way around." It went on to say that "the rancor and suspicion between parties has gotten worse instead of better."

Citizens' right to information was hampered by the government. According to a report by the Associated Press on March 13, 2015, authorities were undermining the laws that were supposed to guarantee citizens' right to information and the systems created to give citizens information about their government. In addition, it was getting harder to use public records to hold government officials accountable (www.ap.org, March 13, 2015). An article on the website of the CNN reported on February 13, 2015 that journalists and news supervision authorities had continually slammed the current U.S. administration as one of the least transparent. At least 15 journalists were arrested in Ferguson protests (edition.cnn.com, February 13, 2015).

III. Economic and Social Rights under Challenge

In 2015, no substantial progress concerning the economic and social rights of U.S. citizens were made. Workers carried out mass strikes to claim their rights at work. Food-insecure and homeless populations remained huge. Many U.S. people suffered from poor health.

The rights of laborers at work were not effectively protected. On October 6, 2015, Al Jazeera America reported that about 40 percent of private-sector workers, or 44 million people in America, did not have access to paid sick leave. Large scale strikes in many industries were reported. In February 2015, workers at nine oil refineries in California, Texas, Kentucky and Washington states carried out strikes, protesting onerous overtime, unsafe staffing levels and dangerous conditions (america.aljazeera.com, February 2, October 6, 2015). In April, the same year, fast food workers walked off the job in 230 cities, staging a strike aimed at a minimum wage of 15 U.S. dollars. In November, they walked out in hundreds of cities for the same reason. About 2,000 workers at seven major U.S. airports went on strike in November to protest low wages (thinkprogress.org, April 15, 2015; www.usatoday.com, November 10, November 19, 2015).

There was huge income gap between the rich and the poor. In the United States, 3.1 percent of income earned annually went to the poorest 20 percent of people, while 51.4 percent was earned by the richest 20 percent (www.usatoday.com, October 10, 2015). Official data showed that 46.7 million people were living in poverty in 2014. (www.census.gov). In Delaware, the percentage of people living below the federal poverty line in 2014 was 12.5 percent, creeping up from 11.7 percent in 2013. Nearly a quarter of residents of Wilmington, Delaware lived below the poverty line. The poverty rate for children was around 20 percent. U.S. people were pessimistic about the prospects of social and economic instability. Seventy-nine percent of Americans believed it was more common for people to fall out of the middle class than rise up to it (www.usatoday.com, June 9, November 23, 2015).

There was a large food-insecure population in the United States. According to a report published on *the Guardian* website on November 26, 2015, government statistics suggested that between 2008 and 2014 at least 48.1 million people a year were classed as "food insecure", including 19.2 percent of all households with children, meaning they could not always afford to eat balanced meals (www.theguardian.com, November 26, 2015). The U.S. Centers for Disease Control and Prevention (CDC) estimated that each year, 48 million people suffered from a foodborne illness, resulting in 128,000 hospitalizations and 3,000 deaths (www.pewtrusts.org, December 4, 2015). Approximately one fifth of all U.S. children lived in food-insecure households, according to the most recent data from the U.S. Department of Agriculture (america.aljazeera.com, October 8, 2015).

Hundreds of thousands of U.S. people were homeless. A report published on *the USA Today* website on June 9, 2015 said housing prices had skyrocketed in the United States in recent years, while income levels remained stagnant. Fifty-five percent of Americans had made more financial sacrifice to afford their housing. According to a report by the National Association of Realtors, the gap between rental costs and household income had been widening to unsustainable levels (www.usatoday.com, June 9, July 31, 2015). A study by the U.S. Department of Housing and Urban Development (HUD) found that more than 560,000 people were homeless in the United States as of November 18, 2015. About one fourth of them were children under the age of 18 (www.hud.gov). In New York City, there were 59,568 homeless people, including 14,361 homeless families with 23,858 homeless children, sleeping each night in municipal shelters in October 2015, 86 percent higher than the number in 2005. People living on streets had no access to toilets or showers (www.pewtrusts.org, November 11, 2015). In recent years, Los Angeles, Seattle, Portland and the state of Hawaii have all recently declared emergencies over the rise of homelessness (www.presstv.ir, November 20, 2015).

Human right to health of U.S. people was not fully protected. According to a report of the Institute for Policy Innovation released on September 18, 2015, there were still 33 million people in the United States uninsured, although U.S. Congress had passed the health care reform bill in 2010, promising to establish a universal healthcare system (www.ipi.org, September 18, 2015). The United States was reported to have the worst medical care system and the highest number of infant mortalities out of 11 developed countries (borgenproject.org, August 23, 2015). There were more than 6,200 places nationwide with a shortage of primary care physicians (www.washingtonpost.com, December 12, 2015). Today, more than 1.2 million people in the United States were HIV-positive. About one in eight of those infected were unaware of their status (edition.cnn.com, December 9, 2015). There was a significant difference between the health conditions of the rich and the poor. According to an AFP report on October 14, 2015, in Brooklyn's poorest neighborhood of Brownsville, New York City, nearly 40 percent of its citizens lived below the federal poverty level. Brownsville suffered more than twice the rates of new HIV diagnoses in New York City. Its people died 11 years earlier than those living around Manhattan's financial district (AFP, October 14, 2015).

Case fatality rate due to drug overdose set new record high. According to a CDC report, drug overdose was the leading cause of diseases in the United States. The death rate from drug overdose more than doubled from 6.0 per 100,000 population in 1999 to 13.8 in 2013. More than 47,000 people died from drug overdoses in 2014, an increase of 3,018 from 2013. Heroin poses the biggest issue among all forms of drug overdose.

In 2013, deaths from heroin-related overdose exceeded 8,200, nearly quadrupling that of 2002. In 2014, the number surged to 10,574. Increasing number of young people and females took heroin. Compared with figures in the period from 2002 to 2004, the number of young heroin addicts aged between 18 and 25 in 2011-2013 period increased by 109 percent, while female users doubled (www.cdc.gov, October 16, December 29, 2015; www.usnews.com, December 18, 2015).

IV. Racial Discrimination Worse Than Ever

In 2015, racial relations in the United States kept deteriorating. Law enforcement and justice fields were heavily influenced by racial discrimination, and race-based hate crimes occurred occasionally. Anti-Muslim remarks caused a great clamor, and minority races were unable to change their vulnerable status in economic and social lives.

Americans' view of race relations was at a two-decade low. A poll jointly released by the CBS News and *The New York Times* on May 4, 2015 showed that 61 percent of Americans characterized race relations in the United States as "bad," including a majority of white and black respondents. The figure was the highest since 1992 (newyork.cbslocal.com, May 4, 2015). A *Wall Street Journal*-NBC News poll in December 2015 showed that only 34 percent of Americans believe race relations in the United States were fairly good or very good, down from a high of 77 percent in January 2009 (blogs.wsj.com, December 16, 2015). A survey released in November 2015 by the Public Religion Research

Institute in the United States showed that 35 percent of Americans believed racial tensions were a major concern in their own communities, jumping 18 percentage points from 2012 (publicreligion.org, November 17, 2015). Figures released in August 2015 by Pew Research Center showed that 50 percent of Americans said that racism was a big problem in the U.S. society; 60 percent Americans said the country needed to continue making changes to achieve racial equality, up 14 percentage points from a year ago (www.people-press.org, August 5, 2015).

Cases of African-Americans being killed by police occurred repeatedly. On November 15, 2015, the 24-year-old African-American Jamar Clark was shot dead by white police officers. The fatal shooting occurred when two police officers were trying to arrest him. Witnesses said that Clark was handcuffed when he was shot in the head. The civil rights organization "Black Lives Matter" organized protests in multiple cities across the country. In a Facebook post, Black Lives Matter activists noted "the era of white supremacist terrorism against people of color across the U.S.," (www.theatlantic.com, November 18, 2015; www.mprnews.org, November 20, 2015; www.huffingtonpost.com, November 24, 2015) On April 12, 2015, as 25-year-old African-American Freddie Gray was being arrested, police handcuffed him and had knees on his back and his head. Gray was dragged and thrown into the back of a police van with his face down. Gray requested medical attention while being transported in the van but the request was denied. Gray lapsed into a coma following the journey on April 12 and died a week later in a hospital. He died of a severe spinal cord injury. The incident sparked large-scale protests in Baltimore. The protests turned violent on April 27, and Maryland Gov. Larry Hogan declared a state of emergency and activated the National Guard. It was the second time in six months that a state called out the National Guard to enforce order after a white police officer killed a black teenager, Michael Brown, in Ferguson in 2014. *The New York Times* said that Gray had become the nation's latest symbol of police brutality in an April 28 story. (edition.cnn.com, April 29, 2015; www.bbc.com, May 5, 2015; baltimore.cbslocal.com, April 27, 2015; www.nytimes.com, April 27 and 28, 2015) According to *The Washington Post* website, police fatally shot 965 people in 2015 as of December 24, 2015, including 36 unarmed African-Americans (www.washingtonpost.com, December 24, 2015). The CBS News-*New York Times* poll released on May 4, 2015 showed that 79 percent of African-Americans believed police were more likely to use deadly force against a black person than against a white person, and black respondents were more likely than white respondents to believe their local police made them feel anxious rather than safe (newyork.cbslocal.com, May 4, 2015). According to a poll released by the National Bar Association in the United States, 88 percent of blacks believed black people were treated unfairly by police, compared with 59 percent of whites who shared that view (www.usatoday.com, September 9, 2015).

Racial discrimination in the criminal justice system was severe. A Gallup survey in 2015 showed that 68 percent of

African-Americans believed the American criminal justice system was racially biased, while 37 percent of whites said the same (www.usatoday.com, June 18, 2015). According to a survey released by the Public Religion Research Institute, 51 percent of Americans disagreed that blacks and other minorities received equal treatment as whites in the criminal justice system, and 78 percent of black Americans disagreed that blacks and other minorities received equal treatment to whites in the criminal justice system (publicreligion.org, May 7, 2015). Prosecutors intentionally struck black people from juries in trials of black defendants. In the South, the practice for prosecutors to strike jurors based on race remained common (www.newyorker.com, June 5, 2015).

Race-related hate crimes occurred occasionally. Craig Stephen Hicks, 46, shot dead three Muslim students near the University of North Carolina on February 10, 2015. Hicks had frequently posted messages critical of various religions on the Internet (indianexpress.com, June 5, 2015). On June 17, 2015, Dylann Roof, a 21-year-old white man, opened fire and killed nine people, including a pastor, at an African-American church in Charleston in South Carolina. According to witnesses, Roof told the victims, "You rape our women and you're taking over our country, and you have to go." (www.cbsnews.com, June 17, 2015; www.bbc.com, June 19, 2015)

Anti-Muslim remarks caused a great clamor. *The Guardian* reported on November 19, 2015 that a Republican presidential candidate made public comments, saying that he would consider warrantless searches of Muslims and increased surveillance of mosques, and that he would not rule out tracking Muslim Americans in a database or giving them "a special form of identification that noted their religion (www.theguardian.com, November 19, 2015)." On December 7, the presidential candidate made a statement calling for "a total and complete shutdown of Muslims entering the United States (www.economist.com, December 8, 2015)." In recent years, Americans' view on Islam became more and more negative. According to a survey by the Public Religion Research Institute, 56 percent of Americans said that the values of Islam were "at odds" with America's values and way of life, and 76 percent of Republicans were especially likely to have the same opinion (www.washingtonpost.com, November 17, 2015). The Human Rights Committee remained concerned about the practice of racial profiling and surveillance by law enforcement officials targeting certain ethnic minorities, notably Muslims (daccess-dds-ny.un.org).

Minority races were in a dire situation. According to figures from the Bureau of Labor Statistics, U.S. Department of Labor, the unemployment rates in November 2015 were 4.3 percent for whites, 9.4 percent for blacks and 6.4 percent for Hispanics. The unemployment rate for blacks more than doubled that for whites, and the figure for Hispanics was 50 percent higher than that for whites (www.bls.gov). The unemployment rate for black college graduates was roughly equal to the rate for white Americans with associate degrees (huffingtonpost.com, December 18, 2015). A third of Iowa's black households earned less than 20,000 U.S. dollars annually, compared with 8 percent of white households. More than one fifth of white households in Iowa earned 100,000 U.S. dollars or more in a year, but only eight percent of black households did (www.usatoday.com, October 31, 2015). Approximately 57 percent of New York City homeless shelter residents were African-American, 31 percent were Latino, 8 percent were white (www.coalitionforthehomeless.org, March 18, 2015). According to a CNN report on February 18, 2015, financial inequality was pervading the country and it was getting worse. Whites had 12 times the wealth of blacks and nearly 10 times more than Hispanics. "The American Dream remains out of reach for many African-American and Hispanic families." (money.cnn.com, February 18, 2015) The documentary Seeking Asylum by African-American Darnell Walker triggered heated responses after debuting online, chronicling the plight of black Americans who no longer felt safe in the United States due to rampant police brutality and were looking to settle elsewhere. Miles Marshall Lewis, who moved to France in 2004 from the United States, published his book "No Country for Black Men" in 2014, a response to the wave of police killings targeting blacks (www.thedailybeast.com, November 11, 2015).

V. Missing Rights for Women and Children

Rights of women and children were grossly violated in the United States in 2015. Women were facing serious workplace discrimination, domestic violence and sexual violation and children were under the threats of arms, abuse, poverty and police violence.

Women were facing worsening situation of inferior social status. On December 11, 2015, the United Nations Working Group on the issue of discrimination against women in law and in practice delivered a statement after a mission to the United States and pointed out the missing rights and protections such as universal paid maternity leave, accessible reproductive health care and equal opportunity in standing for political election for the country's women. In the United States, women fell behind international standards as regards their public and political representation, their economic and social rights and their health and safety protections. Women's average representation in state legislatures was 24.9 percent. This rate placed the country at only the 72nd in global ranking. The gender wage gap was 21 percent. The percentage of women in poverty increased over the past decade, from 12.1 percent to 14.5 percent, with a higher rate of poverty than men. Poor and immigrant women faced severe barriers in accessing sexual and reproductive health services. Women faced fatal consequences of lack of gun control, in particular in cases of domestic violence. The statement also expressed concerns over violence against women in detention as well as the alarming high rates of violence against Native-American women (www.ohchr.org, December 11, 2015).

Women were suffering workplace discrimination. A report released by the U.S. Census Bureau in September 2015 revealed that women in the U.S. were paid 79 cents for every dollar paid to men in 2014, amounting to a yearly wage gap of 10,762 U.S. dollars between full-time working men and women (www.

census.gov). The United Nations' International Labour Organization said in 2014 that out of the 185 countries and territories with available data, the United States was the only industrialized nation with no overall law for cash benefits provided to women during maternity leave (abcnews.go.com, May 6, 2015). A report at the website of *the Los Angeles Times* on May 6, 2015 said that white men had a 42 percent advantage over white women when it came to being promoted to the executive level in U.S. tech companies, but that paled in comparison to the 260 percent advantage they had to Asian women (www.latimes.com, May 6, 2015).

Women fell victim to various forms of sex harassments and sex assaults. A survey released by the Association of American Universities in September 2015 indicated that 23 percent of undergraduate women said they were victims of non-consensual sexual contact and that 20 percent of students said sexual assault and misconduct was very or extremely problematic on their own campus (www.latimes.com, September 21, 2015; www.washingtonpost.com, September 1/September 21, 2015). According to a report at *the USA Today* website on August 17, 2015, a total of 37 percent of women said they had experienced some kind of online harassment. A total of 54 percent of Hispanics and 51 percent of African Americans said they had experienced online harassment. Also, women were more likely to be targets of serious cases in which they were stalked and sexually harassed (www.usatoday.com, August 17, 2015). Another article at *the USA Today* website on December 11, 2015 reported that Daniel

Holtzclaw, a former Oklahoma City police officer, was convicted of sexually assaulting women he preyed upon in a low-income neighborhood he patrolled. He was convicted of 18 counts connected to eight women, all of whom were black (www.usatoday.com, December 11, 2015).

Children were under the threats of guns. According to statistics from the Gun Violence Archive website, as of December 28, 2015, gun-related incidents that year left 682 children under the age of 11 and 2,640 children aged between 12 and 17 killed or injured (www.gunviolencearchive.org, December 28, 2015). The RT America reported at its website on October 10, 2015 that the number of U.S. school shootings that year climbed to 52. There were at least two school shootings a month in 2015 (www.rt.com, October 10, 2015). A report at the website of *the USA Today* on January 21, 2015 said that almost two children were killed every week in unintentional shootings, and nearly two thirds of these unintended deaths took place in a home or vehicle that belonged to the victim's family (www.usatoday.com, January 22, 2015). More than a quarter of the teenagers – 15 years old and up – who died of injuries in the United States were killed in gun-related incidents, according to the American Academy of Pediatrics (www.theatlantic.com, January 12, 2015).

Poor health and living conditions for children. The U.S. Centers for Disease Control and Prevention reported that the rate of newborns with syphilis jumped 38 percent between 2012 and 2014 to its highest level in more than a decade (www.washingtonpost.com, November 12, 2015). A survey said that one in five drug abusers in some treatment programs in the United States received their first taste of these illegal substances from their parents, usually before the age of 18 (abcnews.go.com, August 24, 2015). According to U.S. Census Bureau, about 17.4 million children under the age of 18 were being raised without a father and 45 percent lived below the poverty line (singlemotherguide. com, June 1, 2015). About 6 percent of New York City's African-American population under 18 years old and nearly 3 percent Latino children utilized New York City shelters because of homelessness (www.coalitionforthehomeless.org, March 19, 2015). *The USA Today* website reported on August 15, 2015 that 47 percent of rural Hispanic babies were born poor, compared to 41 percent of Hispanic babies in urban areas. Hispanics babies born in rural enclaves were more likely to be impoverished and it was harder for them to receive help from federal and state programs, such as the Special Supplemental Nutrition Program for Women, Infants and Children. "These babies are starting behind the starting line." (www.usatoday.com, August 15, 2015)

Children were suffering abuse. A report at the website of *The Washington Post* on January 1, 2015 said that among the young children killed in the D.C. region, the majority was killed by a parent or guardian (www.washingtonpost.com, January 1, 2015). *The Miami Herald* website on March 10, 2015 reported that one in three girls and one in five boys would become a victim of child sexual abuse in Florida before they turned 18. Such experience would have serious negative impact on their future lives. On average, each victim of child sexual abuse would lose

250,000 U.S. dollars in earnings throughout his or her lifetime because of the abuse. Fifty percent of victims had below-average grades (www.miamiherald.com, March 10, 2015).

African-American children fell victim to police violence. The CNN website on June 10, 2015 reported that a video went viral online showing violence by a white police officer of the Police Department in McKinney, Texas, against a 14-year-old African-American girl. The officer, called to a community swimming pool party after complaints, cursed at several black teenagers and yanked the girl wearing only a bikini to the ground. He also pointed his gun at the teenagers. The white witness who shot the video said there was no doubt race was a factor in how police responded. This incident triggered some public protests (edition.cnn.com, June 10, 2015). On October 26, 2015, a video that showed Ben Fields, a white school resource officer at Spring Valley High School in South Carolina, manhandling an African-American school girl drew intense criticism. The officer grabbed the girl, who used her cell phone during class, by the neck, flipped her over and dragged her across the floor. Fields in 2013 was named as a defendant in a federal lawsuit that claimed he "unfairly and recklessly targets African-American students." The U.S. National Association for the Advancement of Colored People criticized that such violence "doesn't affect white students". Victoria Middleton, the executive director for the South Carolina branch of the American Civil Liberties Union, said that regardless of the reason for the officer's actions, such egregious use of force – against young people who were sitting in their classrooms – was outrageous. "School should be a place to learn and grow, not a place to be brutalized." (abcnews.go.com, October 28, 2015)

VI. Gross Violations of Human Rights in Other Countries

In 2015, the United States continued to trample on human rights in other countries, causing tremendous civilian casualties. Its overseas monitoring projects infringed on the privacy of citizens of other countries while torture scandals at the Guantanamo Bay detention camp continued. Up to date, the United States has not ratified some core human rights conventions of the United Nations and voted against some important human rights resolutions.

Air strikes caused a large number of civilian casualties. According to Airwars, a project aimed at tracking air strikes in the Middle East, the United States had repeatedly organized coalition forces to launch air strikes against military forces in Iraq and Syria since August 8, 2014. As of December 6, 2015, the United States launched 3,965 air strikes in Iraq and 2,823 in Syria, causing an estimated number of civilian deaths between 1,695 and 2,239 (www.airwars.org). The Syrian government called U.S.-led coalition air strikes an "act of aggression" (www.independent.co.uk, December 7, 2015). On October 3, 2015, a hospital run by aid group "Doctors Without Borders" in the city of Kunduz in Afghanistan was under a bombing that continued for half an hour. Many patients who were unable to move were killed on site, while some staff of the aid group were shot at from the air while fleeing the hospital. A total of 42 people were killed in the air strike, with some bodies charred beyond recognition (www.sputniknews.com, December 12, 2015; www.abcnews.go.com, October 5, 2015).

A frequent use of drones claimed many innocent lives. According to an October 15, 2015 report run by Daily Mail website, when carrying out drone assassinations, the U.S. military used "phone data alone" – a limited way of guaranteeing a kill. During Operation Haymaker, a campaign in northeastern Afghanistan which ran between January 2012 and February 2013, some 219 people were killed by drones but just 35 were the intended targets. During another five-month stretch of the operation, a staggering 90 percent of those killed were not the intended target. Despite this all the deaths were labeled EKIA, or "enemy killed in action." (www.dailymail.co.uk, October 15, 2015). A report posted on April 24, 2015 by *The Washington Post* on its website said a study, which documented 415 strikes in Pakistan and Yemen since the September 11, 2001 attacks, put the total number of killed civilians between 423 and 962 (www.washingtonpost.com, April 24, 2015). The abuse of drone strikes not only drew widespread criticism from international community, but also incurred strong doubt from U.S. scholars. *The Washington Post* posted an article on March 20, 2015, introducing to its readers two books on drones – Kill Chain: The Rise of the High-Tech Assassins, by Andrew Cockburn, and A Theory of the Drones, by Gregoire Chamayou. Cockburn sees America's killer drone policy as "the culmination of a historical pattern of lies, deception and greed in the deployment of lethal military force around the world" and as "a continuation of previous U.S. assassination policy." Failing miserably to achieve the country's stated goal of enhanced security, the policy simultaneously undermined the democratic process, Cockburn writes, noting that "assassination by robot is bound to inspire rather than curtail extremism." According to Chamayou and Cockburn, killer drone exposes the trend toward a new – and "inhumane form of warfare." "With drone warfare, there is no victory, just perpetual elimination." (www.washingtonpost.com, March 20, 2015).

Abuse of cruel torture trampled on human rights. A report by the U.S. Senate on the study of the Central Intelligence Agency's detention and interrogation program found that the CIA's use of brutal interrogation techniques, such as waterboarding, long-term solitary confinement, slamming prisoners' heads into walls, lashing and death threat, were in serious violation of U.S. law (www.intelligence.senate.gov). While according to some witnesses, the CIA torture went far beyond the Senate report had disclosed. Majid Khan, a Guantanamo Bay detainee-turned government cooperating witness, said interrogators poured ice water on his genitals, twice videotaped him naked and repeatedly touched his "private parts." At one point, Khan said, his feet and lower legs were placed in tall boot-like metal cuffs that dug into his flesh and immobilized his legs. The guards also stripped him naked, hung him from a wooden beam for three days and provided him with water but no food. All the above torture details that Khan had undergone were not included in the Senate report (www.theguardian.com, June 2, 2015). On January 11, 2016, human rights experts, including the UN special rapporteurs on torture Juan E. Mendez; on human rights and counterterrorism, Ben Emmerson; on independence of the judiciary, Monica Pinto; Chair-Rapporteur of the UN Working Group on Arbitrary Detention Seong-Phil Hong; and the director of the Office for Democratic Institutions and Human Rights under the Organization for Security and Co-operation in Europe, Michael Georg Link, together called on the U.S. Government to promptly close the Guantanamo Bay detention facility, 14 years after the detention center became operational. The experts recalled in the letter that close to 100 detainees still languished in Guantanamo after years of arbitrary detention without trial (www.un.org, January 11, 2016).

The United States spied on leaders from other countries. The BBC reported on April 30, 2015 that the U.S. National Security Agency, by working with other secret services, has long monitored on European leaders (www.bbc.com, April 30, 2015). *The Independent* reported on June 24, 2015 that the United States had bugged the phones of three French presidents and many other senior French officials, for which a French government spokesman said was "unacceptable" (www.independent.co.uk, June 24, 2015). Facing criticism from its allies, the U.S. government continued to monitor some leaders in the name of "national security purpose" (www.theguardian.com, December 30, 2015).

Though the United States repeatedly vowed to defend "human rights," it still has not ratified core human rights conventions of the UN, including *the International Covenant on Economic, Social and Cultural Rights*; *the Convention on the Elimination of all Forms of Discrimination against Women*; *the Convention on the Rights of the Child* and *the Convention on the Rights of Persons with Disabilities*. The United States is the only country that is yet to ratify *the Convention on the Rights of the Child*. The United States also takes an uncooperative attitude towards international human rights issues. It often kept stalling or turned a deaf ear to criticisms leveled by the UN Human Rights Council special sessions and High Commissioners for Human Rights. On September 28, 2015 when the UN Human Rights Council adopted a resolution related to development right, the United States, as always, voted against it (www.un.org).

Chronology of Human Rights Violations of the United States in 2015

JANUARY

Jan. 3

The Washington Post website reported that John Paul Quintero, an unarmed 23-year-old Hispanic man, was shot by police in Wichita, Kansas.

Jan. 6

The Washington Post website reported that Autumn Steele, an unarmed 34-year-old woman, was shot by police in Burlington, Iowa.

On the same day, the website reported that Leslie Sapp III, a 47-year-old black man, was shot by police in Knoxville, Pennsylvania.

Jan. 8

The Washington Post website reported that Artago Damon Howard, an unarmed 36-year-old black man, was shot by police in a parking lot in Strong, Arkansas.

Jan. 12

The Atlantic magazine's website reported that according to the American Academy of Pediatrics, more than a quarter of the teenagers – 15 years old and up – who died of injuries in the United States were killed in gun-related incidents.

Jan. 13

The Washington Post website reported that Richard McClendon, a 43-year-old mentally-ill man, was shot by police in his mother's home in Jourdanton, Texas.

Jan. 14

The Washington Post website reported that Talbot Schroeder, a 75-year-old man, was shot by police in a house in Old Bridge, New Jersey, for refusing repeated commands from a police officer to drop the knife.

Jan. 16

"No Freshness in our 2016 presidential contest," an article published on the website of *The Washington Post* said the likely slate of candidates will include the son of a governor and presidential candidate, the son of a congressman and presidential candidate, the wife of a president and the brother of a president, son of a president and grandson of senator. Family pedigree and prestige were dominating factors swaying politics.

Jan. 22

The websites of *The Huffington Post* and *The USA Today* reported that 10 former McDonald's workers from Virginia sued their stores for racial discrimination and sexual harassment. They said they suffered racial discrimination from the managers from time to time and alleged they were wrongfully fired last year and replaced with mostly white workers because their managers believed there had been "too many black people [working] in the store."

Jan. 29

The Washington Post website reported that Ralph Willis, an unarmed 42-year-old man, was shot by police in Stillwater, Oklahoma, for making a threatening gesture toward a police officer.

Jan. 31

The Washington Post website reported that Edward Donnell Bright, a 54-year-old mentally-ill black man, was shot by police outside a 7-Eleven in Baltimore, Maryland.

FEBRUARY

Feb. 1

The website of Al Jazeera America reported that about 3,800 oil refinery workers at nine oil refineries in California, Texas, Kentucky and Washington states carried out strikes, protesting onerous overtime, unsafe staffing levels and dangerous working conditions that the industry kept ignoring. The strike leaders said the possible occurrence of fires, emissions, leaks and explosions every day had threatened local communities, while the industry did nothing about it.

Feb. 2

The Washington Post website reported that a police officer in Hummelstown, Pennsylvania, shocked David Kassick, an unarmed 59-year-old man, with a Taser and then shot him twice in the back as he lay on the ground.

On the same day, London-based Bureau of Investigative Journalism released a study which said at least 2,464 people had been killed by U.S. drone strikes outside the country's declared war zones since 2009. The research also showed there had been nearly nine times more strikes in the current U.S. administration in Pakistan, Yemen and Somalia than there were under his predecessor.

Feb. 4

The Washington Post website reported that Jeremy Lett, an unarmed 28-year-old black man, was shot five times by a police officer in Tallahassee, Florida.

Feb. 8

The Washington Post website reported that the incumbent U.S. president said in a video aired during the Grammy Awards 2015 that nearly one in five women in the United States had experienced rape or attempted rape.

Feb. 10

The Washington Post website reported that Antonio Zambrano-Montes, an unarmed 35-year-old mentally-ill Hispanic man, was shot by three police officers after he threw rocks at vehicles on a street in Pasco, Washington.

On the same day, the Equal Justice Initiative (EJI) released a report on lynchings in the United States, which documented 3,959 racial terror lynchings of African Americans between 1877 and 1950. It said racial terror lynchings of African Americans strengthened racial segregation. The geographic, political, economic and social consequences of decades of terror lynchings can still be seen in many communities today, according to the report.

Feb. 12

The Chicago Tribune reported that more than 100 cases of miscarriage of justice were done by the court in Cook County, Illinois, over the past 25 years. In 1985, a man in the state was arrested for allegedly raping and murdering a woman. Without sufficient evidence, he was forced to admit to the charges after 40 hours of interrogation and was sentenced to life. In February 2015, the DNA test found the man was innocent.

Feb. 13

The CNN reported on its website that press freedom deteriorated since 2009 in the United States. Journalists and news supervision authorities had continually slammed the current U.S. administration, which stubbornly hampered the disclosure of government information, as one of the least transparent. At least 15 journalists were arrested in Ferguson protests.

On the same day, *The Washington Post* website reported that Richard Carlin, an unarmed 35-year-old Hispanic man, was shot by police in a house in Pennsylvania.

Feb. 15

The Washington Post website reported that Lavall Hall, an unarmed 25-year-old mentally-ill black man, was shot by police on a street in Miami Gardens, Florida, after he refused to drop a broomstick handle.

Feb. 18

According to a report on the CNN website, whites had 12 times the wealth of blacks and nearly 10 times more than Hispanics. Some 42 percent of blacks aged 25 to 55 had college loans, compared to 28 percent of whites. "The American Dream remains out of reach for many

African-American and Hispanic families."

Feb. 20

The Washington Post website reported that Ruben Villalpando, an unarmed 31-year-old Hispanic man, was shot by police on a street in Euless, Texas, as he walked toward an officer's patrol car with his hands up.

Feb. 27

The Washington Post website reported that Ernesto Javiar Canepa Diaz, an unarmed 27-year-old Hispanic man, was shot by police in a vehicle in Santa Ana, California.

Feb. 28

The Washington Post website reported that Deven Guilford, an unarmed 17-year-old male, was shot seven times by police on a street in Roxand Township, Michigan, during an altercation with a police officer.

On the same day, the website reported that Thomas Allen, an unarmed 34-year-old black man, was shot by police in St Louis, Missouri, during an altercation with a police officer.

MARCH

March 1

The Washington Post website reported that Charly Leundeu Keunang, an unarmed 43-year-old homeless black man, was shot by police on a street in Los Angeles, California, in an altercation with police officers patrolling Skid Row.

March 4

The USA Today website reported that the U.S. Department of Justice found through review that police in Ferguson, Mississippi, commonly had racial discrimination. They used force against African Americans inappropriately. The record of Ferguson police showed that in 88 percent of cases in which Ferguson documented the use of force, those actions were used against African Americans. A review of 161 such cases by Justice investigators found that none of the incidents resulted in disciplinary action.

March 6

The website of *the U.S. News & World Report* quoted a researcher of the National Gang Center as saying that in the past five years the United States had seen an 8 percent increase in the number of gangs, an 11 percent increase in members and a 23 percent increase in gang-related homicides.

March 13

The Associated Press reported that it was getting harder and more expensive to use public records to hold government officials accountable. Authorities were undermining the laws that are supposed to guarantee citizens' right to information, turning the right to know into just plain "no."

March 16

"The Best 'Democracy' Money Can Buy," an article published on the website of Zerohedge, said that between 2007 and 2012 in the United States, 200 most politically active corporations spent a combined 5.8 billion U.S. dollars on federal lobbying and campaign contributions. They got 4.4 trillion U.S. dollars in federal business and support in return.

On the same day, a *USA Today* report said the U.S. government did a bad job in implementing legislation on freedom of information. Though the laws were well written, the public record revealed that it was fairly difficult to obtain information from key departments.

March 19

The Washington Post website reported that Brandon Jones, an unarmed 18-year-old black man, was shot by police on a street in Cleveland, Ohio, as he came out of a grocery store that he had broken into.

March 20

A *USA Today* report, which was published on its website, said the nation had its lowest midterm-election voter turnout in 2014 since the 1940s.

The average turnout across the United States was 37 percent, with a low of 28.8 percent recorded in Indiana. Only seven states saw more than half of their voters cast ballots in the election.

On the same day, *The Washington Post* said on its website that since 9/11, more than 500 drone strikes had killed nearly 4,000 individuals. Drone operators, called the "stick monkeys," had trouble distinguishing women and children from the high-value targets they were seeking.

March 26

A report on *the Time* magazine's website quoted an investigation by the BBC as saying that tens of thousands of children were sexually exploited each year in the United States. Hundreds of U.S. children were sold into sex, according to the BBC. Poverty and neglect were thought to be some of the main reasons why children were vulnerable to sex trafficking.

APRIL

April 2

The Washington Post website reported that Eric Harris, an unarmed 44-year-old black man, was shot on a street in Tulsa, Oklahoma, as a police officer inadvertently fired a gun at him.

April 8

A report from *USA Today* website said the U.S. government started keeping secret records of Americans' international telephone calls nearly a decade before the Sept. 11 terrorist attacks, harvesting billions of calls.

April 9

The Fox News reported on its website that as a punishment, a 50-year-old mentally-ill inmate Darren Rainey was taken to the showers for nearly two hours with the water reportedly rigged to a scalding 180 degrees Fahrenheit. Corrections officers even taunted Rainey, asking him how he liked his shower. He was finally scalded to death.

April 12

Freddie Gray, a 25-year-old African-American man, was arrested in Baltimore on April 12. He died later while in police custody. His death, reportedly a result of inappropriate behavior by police, sparked large-scale "Justice for Freddie" protests. A curfew was instituted, and the National Guard was brought in.

April 15

Reuters reported that Walter Scott, an unarmed African-American man, was fatally shot in the back by a white police officer in North Charleston, South Carolina, on April 4. In March, an unarmed black teen Tony Robinson Jr. was shot by a white police officer in Wisconsin, triggering a series of demonstrations. The demonstrators protested against the use of lethal weapons against minorities.

On the same day, Think Progress reported on its website that fast food workers walked off the job in 230 cities on April 15, staging the largest-ever strike in their movement aimed at a 15 dollar minimum wage and the right to form a union.

April 21

The Washington Post website reported that Daniel Covarrubias, an unarmed 37-year-old man, was shot by police in Lakewood, Washington.

April 25

The Washington Post website reported that David Felix, an unarmed 24-year-old black man, was shot by police in an apartment building in New York.

MAY

May 4

A poll jointly released by the CBS News and *the New York Times* showed that 61 percent of Americans characterized race relations in the United States as "bad." The figure was the highest since 1992.

May 5

The Washington Post website reported that Brendon Glenn, an unarmed and homeless 29-year-old black man, was shot by police outside a bar in Venice, California.

May 6

According to a report by the ABC News, figures released by the International Labor Organization showed that the United States is only one of three countries in the world that don't offer paid maternity leave.

May 7

According to a survey released by the Public Religion Research Institute, 51 percent of Americans disagreed that blacks and other minorities receive equal treatment as whites in the criminal justice system, and 78 percent of black Americans disagreed that blacks and other minorities receive equal treatment to whites in the criminal justice system.

May 11

The United States was reviewed for the second time on its human rights records through the Universal Periodic Review of the UN Human Rights Council on May 11. Several reports produced as part of the review revealed that more problems concerning torture, death penalty and other fields existed in the United States, which was a sharp contrast with the country's claim of improved human rights. Many nations criticized the U.S. reluctance to sign the human rights treaties. The UN has set up nine core human rights conventions, six of them are still awaiting the country's ratification. The United States portrays itself as the global leader in human rights, but fails to safeguard the economic, social and cultural rights listed in international human rights instruments.

May 13

The Washington Post website reported that a mentally-ill female prisoner, Natasha McKenna, died after she was shot four times with a Taser stun gun by a guard in the Fairfax County jail three months ago. Her hands and feet were shackled when she was shot.

May 19

The Washington Post website reported that Alfredo Rials-Torres, an unarmed 54-year-old Hispanic man, was shot by police in an apartment in Arlington, Virginia.

May 22

The CNN website reported that in a complaint filed with the U.S. Departments of Education and Justice, a coalition of more than 60 Asian-American organizations claimed that Harvard unfairly held Asian-American applicants to a higher standard.

May 26

The BBC website reported that the Mapping Police Violence project showed that black people are three times more likely to be killed by police in the United States than white people.

May 28

A *New York Times* article cited a report as saying that racial residential segregation has become a way of life in the United States. About one third of African-Americans live in severe segregation, with Baltimore, Philadelphia and New York City among the cities suffering the most severe racial segregation.

May 29

A report released by the Pew Research Center shows that a majority of Americansopposed the government collecting bulk dataon its citizens. Sixty-one percent of those aware of the U.S. government's surveillance programs said they had become less confident that the programs were serving the public interest.

JUNE

June 1

According to U.S. Census Bureau, about 17.4 million children under the age of 18 are being raised without a father as of June 2015 and 45 percent of them live below the poverty line.

June 2

According to a report posted on the website of *the Guardian*, the CIA used sexual abuses and other forms of torture more extensively than had been disclosed by the Senate report in 2014. Majid Khan, a Guantanamo Bay detainee-turned government cooperating witness, said interrogators poured ice water on his genitals, videotaped him naked, placed his feet and lower legs in tall boot-like metal cuffs that immobilized his legs, hung him naked from a wooden beam for three days and provided him with water but no food. All the above torture details that Khan had undergone were not included in the Senate report.

June 10

According to a report released by the International Trade Union Confederation (ITUC), the United States is one of the world's worst countries that systematically infringed on workers' rights.

On the same day, CNN Money reported on its website that a video showing a white officer with the Police Department in McKinney, Texas, using violence against a 14-year-old African American girl went viral online. A white witness who shot the video said there was no doubt race was a factor in how police responded.

June 11

A Pew Research Center survey showed multiracial American children were discriminated in the United States. Fifty-five percent of multiracial Americans said they had been subjected to racial slurs or jokes.

June 15

The Washington Post website reported that Kris Jackson, an unarmed 22-year-old black man, was shot by police as he tried to climb through a motel room window in South Lake Tahoe, California.

June 17

According to the website of CBS News, Dylann Roof, a 21-year-old white man, opened fire and killed nine people, including a pastor, at an African-American church in Charleston, South Carolina.

June 18

Citing a Gallup survey, *the USA Today* website reported that a drastically greater number of African-Americans now rank race relations as the most important issue facing the country, following the killing of unarmed African-American Michael Brown by law enforcement officers in Ferguson. Sixty-eight percent of African-Americans believe the American criminal justice system is racially biased.

June 24

The website of *the U.S. News and World Report* said in an article that the U.S. education spending as a percentage of all government spending had consistently decreased over the last five years, down to just one percent in 2015 from 1.27 percent in 2011, resulted in an overall 19.8 percent decrease.

On the same day, the British newspaper Independent reported that the United States had bugged the phones of three French presidents and many other senior French officials for a long time. A French government spokesman said this was "unacceptable."

June 25

The Washington Post website reported that Spencer McCain, an unarmed 41-year-old black man, was shot by police in Owings Mills, Maryland.

JULY

July 2

The Washington Post website reported that Victor Emanuel Larosa, an unarmed 23-year-old African-American man, was shot by police in a yard in Jacksonville, Florida.

July 7

The Washington Post website cited the Syrian Observatory for Human Rights as saying that the U.S.-led coalition is responsible for the deaths of 162 civilians, including 51 children and 35 women.

July 10

The USA Today website reported that some top psychologists had helped CIA and Pentagon bolster torture. Two former presidents of the American Psychological Association served as members of a CIA advisory panel. The association's ethics office, led by Stephen Behnke, also obtained a contract to train Pentagon interrogators.

July 12

A BBC website report cited Wikileaks as saying that the United States had been spying on Japanese cabinet officials, banks and companies since at least eight years ago. Wikileaks says the United States was aware of Japan's internal discussions on issues such as trade talks, climate change policy and nuclear and energy policy – as well as the contents of a confidential briefing in Prime Minister Shinzo Abe's residence. Wikileaks had previously released files showing the United States spied on Germany, France and Brazil – like Japan, all allies.

July 14

A Pew Research Center analysis found that children make up a larger share of the United States' impoverished than of the population as a whole – those younger than 18 make up about a quarter of the total population, but make up about a third of all Americans in poverty. African-American and Hispanic-American children in particular are overrepresented.

July 17

The Washington Post website reported that the U.S. civil rights organizations accused North Carolina of limiting the time for early voting, ending same-day registration and banning voters from casting ballots in places other than their home constituencies through legislation. The report said the conduct seriously damaged the electoral rights of the African-American voters.

July 19

The Washington Post website reported that Samuel Debase, an unarmed 43-year-old African-American man, was shot by police in Mt. Auburn, Ohio.

July 28

The Huffington Post reported on its website that former U.S. President Jimmy Carter said in an interview that "Now it's just an oligarchy with unlimited political bribery being the essence of getting the nominations for president or being elected president. And the same thing applies to governors, and U.S. Senators and Congress members. So, now we've just seen a subversion of our political system as a payoff to major contributors, who want and expect, and sometimes get, favors for themselves after the election is over." The preferences of the average American appeared to have only a minuscule, near-zero, statistically non-significant impact upon public policy.

July 31

The Financial Times reported on its website that the U.S. law allows unlimited contributions to super PACs by individuals and corporations, which changed the political landscape of the nation and enabled billionaires and millionaires to donate a huge amount of fund to presidential candidates more effectively. Some affluent families hoped that they can influence the election results via their wealth. The number of donors who contributed more than one million U.S. dollars to presidential candidates would swamp the 2016 presidential race like never before.

On the same day, *the USA Today* website reported that according to a March report by the National Association of Realtors, the gap between rental costs and household income had been widening to unsustainable levels in the United States.

According to a report to the United Nations by Maud de Boer-Buquicchio, the UN Special Rapporteur on the sale of children, child prostitution and child pornography, in the United States, lesbian, gay, bisexual, transgender and intersex youth are disproportionately represented in runaway and homeless youth programs and child welfare systems and 42 percent of them have been sexually exploited.

AUGUST

Aug. 3

In the document on the Effective promotion of the Declaration on the Rights of Persons Belonging to National or Ethnic, Religious and Linguistic Minorities, a report of the United Nations Secretary-General submitted to the seventieth session of the General Assembly, the Human Rights Committee remained concerned about the practice of racial profiling and surveillance by law enforcement officials targeting certain ethnic minorities, notably Muslims. In December 2014, the Special Rapporteur expressed concerns over the decision not to bring to trial the cases of Michael Brown and Eric Garner in the United States.

Aug. 4

According to an article on the website of *the U.S. News and World Report*, since 2010, a total of 21 states had adopted new laws to limit the exercise of suffrage. Some states shortened the time for early voting, while others limited the number of documents identifying one as a lawful voter. A total of 14 states will carry out fresh measures to limit the exercise of suffrage for first time in 2016 presidential election. The voting rights were hit by the vicious competition between the two parties.

On the same day, CNBC Finance said data from the 2015 Trustees of the Social Security and Medicare trust funds report showed that the U.S. social security system was 25.8 trillion U.S. dollars in the red.

On the same day, in a document provided to the UN General Assembly by the UN General Secretary, the UN Human Rights Council expressed concern in relation to systematic practices of torture, ill-treatment or excessive use of force by members of the police or the security forces during arrest and/or interrogation of terroristic suspects. The Committee specifically raised the issue of the lack of a timeline for closure of the Guantanamo Bay facility and called for the transfer, as soon as possible, of detainees designated for transfer.

Aug. 5

Figures released by Pew Research Center showed 53 percent of whites say more needs to be done to achieve racial equality, up 14 percentage points from 2014. Eighty-six percent of African Americans said that changes must continue to be made to achieve racial equality.

Aug. 7

The report of the Special Rapporteur on torture and other cruel, inhuman or degrading treatment or punishment, submitted by Juan E. Mendez to the UN General Assembly said the U.S. Central Intelligence Agency conducted an extraordinary rendition and secret detention program after 11 September 2001, which saw the United States collaborate with some other countries and assist one another in abducting, transferring, extrajudicially detaining and subjecting individuals to torture.

Aug. 12

According to a report submitted by the UN Secretary-General to the Assembly at its seventieth session on the status of *the Convention on the Rights of the Child*, the United States has yet to ratify *the Convention on the Rights of the Child*. The United States is so far the only country that is yet to ratify the convention.

Aug. 15

The USA Today website reported that 47 percent of rural Hispanic-American babies are born poor. The report quoted a Cornell University researcher as saying that "These babies are starting behind the starting line... And their opportunities as they move into adulthood are jeopardized."

Aug. 18

According to a Pew Research Center report, the revenue-expenditure gap in Social Security fund in the United States was projected to be around 84 billion U.S. dollars. It was forecast that Social Security's combined reserves likely would be fully depleted by 2034. The disability-insurance trust fund could run dry as soon as the end of 2016, while the old-age and survivors' fund was expected to be depleted in 2035.

Aug. 23

The United States was reported to have the worst medical care system and the highest number of infant mortalities out of 11 developed countries and it ranked second to last in preventable deaths, said a report published on the Borgen Project website.

Aug. 24

The ABC news website reported that a survey said that one in five drug abusers in some treatment programs in the United States received their first taste of these illegal substances from their parents, usually before the age of 18, and of these 6 percent even used heroin with them.

Aug. 26

A reporter and a photographer of the local CBS television station in Virginia were shot and killed while filming a morning live television report. A manifesto sent to ABC News by the killer revealed that he was motivated by an African-American church shooting happened in June, 2015 in South Carolina that was conducted by a white man.

SEPTEMBER

Sept. 1

According to a report, titled "Crime in the United States 2014," released by the FBI, an estimated 1,165,383 violent crimes occurred nationwide in 2014, of which 63.6 percent were aggravated assaults, 28 percent were robberies, 7.2 percent rapes and 1.2 percent murders. Firearms were used in 67.9 percent of the nation's murders, 40.3 percent of robberies, and 22.5 percent of aggravated assaults in 2014. Nationwide, there were an estimated 8,277,829 property crimes, with the victims of such crimes suffering losses calculated at an estimated 14.3 billion U.S. dollars.

Sept. 9

The USA Today website reported that according to a poll released by the National Bar Association in the United States, 88 percent of African Americans believed African Americans are treated unfairly by police, and 59 percent of whites shared that view.

Sept. 10

The U.S. government had blocked the release of documents detailing the alleged torture of a suspected top Al Qaeda operative held in Guantanamo Bay, said *the Daily Mail of Britain* on its website. Abu Zubaydah, a 44-year-old Saudi national, was captured in 2002 and has been held in Guantanamo since 2006. According to documents released last year, he lost an eye and was waterboarded 83 times in a single month while in the custody of the CIA at Guantanamo Bay. Joe Margulies, Zubaydah's lead defense lawyer, said the CIA declared all the 116 pages of testimony by Zubaydah classified.

Sept. 16

The USA Today website reported that a former employee is suing Microsoft, alleging the technology giant discriminates against women in technical roles. Microsoft policies and practices "systematically violate female technical employees' rights and result in the unchecked gender bias that pervades its corporate culture," charges the lawsuit, which is seeking class action status.

Sept. 18

According to a report released on the Institute for Policy Innovation website, there were still 33 million people in the U.S. uninsured in 2014, although the incumbent U.S. president promised to sign a universal health care bill into law by the end of his first term.

Sept. 21

The Washington Post and *the Los Angeles Times* reported on their websites that a survey released by the Association of American Universities that covered more than 150,000 students at 27 universities showed that more than one in four female undergraduate students say they have been victimized by nonconsensual sexual contact. In California, 29.7 percent of female undergraduates at the University of Southern California reported the most serious sexual misconduct. Nationally, the rate of such misconduct ranged from 13 percent to 30 percent across campuses.

Sept. 22

The Washington Post reported that those who were not Christians found it difficult to run for a post in public office in the United States. And it was more difficult for those who did not have a religious belief. A Pew poll found that of all religion-related groups, atheists and Muslims were viewed the most negatively by Americans.

Sept. 23

The Washington Post website reported that Keith Harrison McLeod, an unarmed 19-year-old African-American man, was shot by police in Reisterstown, Maryland, after they were called to a pharmacy after the man attempted to fill a prescription that had been forged. After a short chase, officers confronted the man.

OCTOBER

Oct. 1

The Guardian reported on its website that observing the current

American politics was like watching a game of money. The 2016 presidential election was almost going to be the most expensive one in history.

Oct. 2

The Chicago Tribune and *the Huffington Post* reported on their websites that on October 1, Christopher Sean Harper-Mercer, a student at Umpqua Community College in Roseburg, Oregon, entered a classroom in the college with a bullet proof vest on and six guns. He opened fire, killing nine people and wounding nine others, before killing himself. It was the 45th shooting at a school in 2015. There have been 142 shootings at schools since December 14, 2012, the date of the shooting at Sandy Hook Elementary.

Oct. 3

According to the CNN and Sputnik News, a hospital run by aid group "Doctors Without Borders" in the city of Kunduz in Afghanistan was bombed by the U.S. military on October 3, causing 42 deaths, including 12 medical staff and three children. The aid group accused the air strike a "war crime" instead of an "error."

Oct. 5

The Washington Post website reported that Omar Ali, an unarmed 27-year-old man, was shot by police in a bar in Akron, Ohio.

Oct. 8

A report by the Al Jazeera America said that approximately one-fifth of all U.S. children live in food-insecure households, according to data from the U.S. Department of Agriculture. As of 2014, 15.4 percent of Americans overall reside in food-insecure households-a total of more than 48 million people.

Oct. 10

The USA Today website reported that in the United States, the gap between the rich and poor jumped dramatically in the 1980s, making upward mobility increasingly difficult for low-income Americans. In the

United States, 3.1 percent of income earned annually went to the poorest 20 percent of people, while 51.4 percent was earned by the richest 20 percent. Statistics showed that over half of all wealth in the United States belonged to the top 3 percent of earners.

On the same day, the BBC and the RT America reported that gunfire broke out on October 9 on the Northern Arizona University and Texas Southern University campuses. With the two shootings on college campuses, the number of U.S. school shootings in 2015 has climbed to 52, with 30 people killed and 53 others injured.

Oct. 14

An AFP report showed that New York was a city of extreme inequality, where people in the poor neighborhood of Brooklyn died 11 years earlier than those living around Wall Street, according to data released on October 14.

Oct. 15

According to a report run by *Daily Mail* website, when carrying out drone assassinations, the U.S. military used "phone data alone" – a limited way of guaranteeing a kill. During Operation Haymaker, a campaign in northeastern Afghanistan which ran between January 2012 and February 2013, some 219 people were killed by drones but just 35, 15 percent, were the intended targets. During another five-month stretch of the operation, a staggering 90 percent of those killed were not the intended target. Despite this all the deaths were labeled EKIA, or "enemy killed in action."

Oct. 22

The AOL website reported that protests were held in many major cities and towns across the United States on October 22 to stop police brutality. The event's organizer posted 5 shocking facts about police brutality in the United States on its website: 1. More than 920 people have been killed by the police in 2015; 2. Black Americans are more than twice likely to be unarmed when killed during police encounters than whites; 3. Native

Americans are the group just as likely as blacks to be killed by law enforcement officers; 4. Excessive force is one of the most common forms of police misconduct; 5. For every 1,000 people killed by police, only one officer is convicted of a crime.

Oct. 23

The U.S. Court of Appeals for the District of Columbia Circuit ruled that Amir Meshal couldn't sue the FBI for illegally detaining, interrogating and torturing him abroad for four months. Meshal claimed FBI agents held him without process or access to counsel, put him in solitary confinement, and threatened him with torture and death, and returned him to the United States after multiple transfers to squalid jails in several countries.

On the same day, the Christian Science Monitor reported on its website that the American Chamber of Commerce, the biggest commercial lobbying group in the nation, planned to play an active role in the 2016 presidential election. The chamber said it would spend 100 million U.S. dollars in 2016 presidential election, compared with 70 million in 2014.

Oct. 31

According to information provided by the Coalition for the Homeless, in recent years, homelessness in New York City had reached the highest levels since the Great Depression of the 1930s. In October 2015, there were 59,568 homeless people, including 14,361 homeless families with 23,858 homeless children, sleeping each night in the New York City municipal shelter system. The number of homeless New Yorkers sleeping each night in municipal shelters was 86 percent higher than it was ten years ago. Each night thousands of unsheltered homeless people slept on New York City streets, in the subway system, and in other public spaces.

NOVEMBER

Nov. 3

The Washington Post website reported that Jeremy Mardis, an unarmed 6-year-old male, was shot by police in Marksville, Las Vegas.

A study released by the Economic Policy Institute on the same day found that in the third quarter of 2015, African American unemployment in the United States is about double the white unemployment rate. The largest racial gap was in the District of Columbia, where African American joblessness is 5.7 times more than whites.

Nov. 10

The USA Today website reported that fast food workers in the United States walked off the job in hundreds of cities on Nov. 10, staging strikes aimed at a minimum wage of 15 U.S. dollars.

Nov. 11

The CNN website reported that a Republican presidential candidate said he would build a "deportation force" to remove 11 million undocumented immigrants from the country. He has also proposed ending birthright citizenship.

On the same day, the Pew Charitable Trusts website reported that since September, Los Angeles, Seattle, Portland, Oregon and the state of Hawaii had all declared states of emergency to tackle a worsening homeless crisis. Los Angeles had about 25,000 homeless people.

Nov. 12

The Washington Post website said that a report released by the U.S. Centers for Disease Control and Prevention revealed that rate of newborns with syphilis jumped 38 percent between 2012 and 2014. The disease was found in 11.6 of every 100,000 births in 2014.

Nov. 15

According to a report on the CNN website, African-American Jamar Clark was shot dead by police early morning. According to witnesses, Clark was handcuffed when one of the cops had his knee in his back and the other cop was straddling him. It is said that Clark was unable to move and he didn't resist.

Nov. 16

According to an FBI's report on 2014 hate crime statistics, the country reported 5,479 hate crime incidents involving 6,418 offenses. There were 5,462 single-bias incidents involving 6,681 victims. A percent distribution of victims by bias type showed that 48.3 percent were targeted because of the offenders' racial bias, and 17.1 percent were targeted because of the offenders' religious bias.

Nov. 17

The Washington Post website reported that, as of the morning of November 17, the governors of 27 states have said that they are opposed to letting Syrian refugees resettle in their states. Some Republican Party lawmakers and presidential contenders have even called for a ban on letting any Syrian Muslim refugees into the United States.

On the same day, a survey by the Public Religion Research Institute revealed that 63 percent of respondents say blacks face a lot of discrimination in the United States, and 56 percent say Hispanics face a lot of discrimination in the country. Also, 70 percent of Americans say there is a lot of discrimination against Muslims and 45 percent say there is a lot of discrimination against women.

Nov. 18

The U.S. News and World Report website reported that researchers found 18 percent of students said they'd been raped while incapacitated before college, and 41 percent of those young women were raped again while incapacitated during their freshman year. The U.S. CDC revealed that one in five women have been raped in their lifetimes, and a majority of victims personally knew their perpetrators.

Nov. 19

The USA Today website reported that about 2,000 airport workers struck overnight from Nov. 18 to Nov. 19 at seven major airports in the United States to protest low wages, demanding a minimum wage of 15 U.S. dollars.

On the same day, *the Guardian* website reported that a Republican presidential candidate said that he would consider warrantless searches of Muslims and increased surveillance of mosques, and that he would not rule out tracking Muslim Americans in a database or giving them a special form of identification that noted their religion.

Nov. 23

The Chicago Tribune reported that nearly 17,000 immigration cases are pending in Chicago's immigration court. The typical case here is already two and a half years old and, on average. So clogged is the Chicago court that some cases aren't being scheduled for hearings until 2020. Among these cases, about 600 cases of children immigration are still pending, leaving families in limbo.

Nov. 24

The CNN website reported that a Chicago police officer, who was charged in African-American Laquan MacDonald's shooting death, had a history of 20 complaints before he gunned down the 17-year-old, but none resulted in discipline. Outraged that it took as long as 13 months to charge the police officer in MacDonald's death, demonstrators took to the street to demand justice in his death.

Nov. 26

According a report published on *the Guardian* website, government statistics suggested that between 2008 and 2014 at least 48.1 million people a year, including 19.2 percent of all households with children, could not always afford to eat balanced meals.

Nov. 30

The Washington Post website reported that a court filing released on Nov. 30 disclosed details of so-called national security letters, which showed that the FBI used special authority to compel Internet firms to hand over user information, including full browsing histories. These letters are used by the FBI to conduct electronic surveillance without the need for court approval.

DECEMBER

Dec. 1

According to *the Guardian* website, 37-year-old Mustafa al-Aziz al-Shamiri had been held without charge indefinitely at Guantanamo since 2002 for 13 years.

Dec. 2

The USA Today website reported that two gunmen opened fire on a festive staff holiday party at a social services center in San Bernardino on this day, killing 14 and injuring 17 others.

Dec. 10

A new Pew Research Center analysis revealed that the American middle class is shrinking due to slow income growth, and the middle class made up 49.9 percent of the U.S. adult population in 2015, down from 61 percent in 1971. This is the first time for the proportion to drop below 50 percent.

Dec. 11

An article at *the USA Today* website reported that Daniel Holtzclaw, a former Oklahoma City police officer, was convicted of sexually assaulting women he preyed upon in a low-income neighborhood he patrolled. He was convicted of 18 counts – four charges of first-degree rape and 14 other counts – connected to eight women, all of whom were black. A probe revealed about 1,000 officers had lost their licenses for sex crimes or other sexual misconduct in a six-year period.

At the end of a 10-day mission to the United States, a UN Working Group on the issue of discrimination against women in law and in practice noted that in 2010 and 2015, in the framework of its Universal Periodic Review, the U.S. government committed to ratify *the Convention on the Elimination of All Forms of Discrimination Against Women* but this commitment has not yet been implemented. In the United States, women fall behind international standards as regards their right protections.

Dec. 12

The BBC website reported that a survey of more than 6,000 hosts in five U.S. cities concluded that names that sounded African-American were about 16 percent less likely to get a positive response to a request for a room when compared against white-sounding names like Brad or Kristen.

Dec. 13

The website of *the Miami Herald* reported that Lowell Correctional Institution, the nation's largest women's prison, was haunted by corruption and sex scandals. Women alleged in complaints, filed between 2011 and May 2015, that the officers pressure inmates to have sex which happens in bathrooms, closets, the laundry and officers' stations.

Dec. 15

According to the website of *Christian Science Monitor*, the U.S. president first promised to close Guantanamo Bay detention camp in 2007. But until December 15, 2015, 107 prisoners still remained in custody. The UN said indefinite imprisonment of detainees without charge or trial violated international law, calling on the United States to close the military prison camp.

Dec. 16

A report carried by the website of *the Miami Herald* disclosed corruption and brutality of Patrick Quercioli, a corrections officer at Lowell Correctional Institution for women. Though he'd been arrested twice, Quercioli managed to persuade the Florida Department of Corrections to hire him in 2004. He was known among prisoners as one of the most menacing officers at the correctional institution. In the past 10 years 57 inmates died in the prison, not accounting those who make it to hospital.

On the same day, a *Wall Street Journal*-NBC News poll in December 2015 showed that only 34 percent of Americans believe race relations in the United States were fairly good or very good, down 43 percentage points from 2009.

On the same day, Airwars reported on its website that between August 8, 2014 and December 16, 2015, 123 air strikes launched by U.S.-led coalition forces caused a number of civilian deaths between 757 and 1,073.

Dec. 17

According to the intercept.com, intelligence agencies in the United States resort to high technology to spy on civilians. A dozens of cellphone surveillance devices such as Stingray and "dirt boxes" were used by intelligence agencies, such as the NSA and the CIA, to eavesdrop on calls and spying on SMS messages. Two systems are touted as having the ability to extract media files, address books and retrieve deleted text messages.

Dec. 18

Drug (mostly prescription painkillers and heroin) overdose deaths hit record numbers, according to a report released by the U.S. Centers for Disease Control and Prevention. More than 47,000 people died from drug overdoses in 2014, an increase of 6 percent from 2013.

Dec. 24

According to sputniknews.com, former Pentagon official and missile expert Theodore Postol said the targeting of civilian populations for annihilation by U.S. nuclear forces in the 1950s continues to this day. "The fact of the matter is that we have targeted populations from the very beginning and do so to this day," he said.

Dec. 27

The Washington Post website reported that 55-year-old black woman Bettie Jones and her 19-year-old neighbor Quintonio LeGrier were "accidentally" shot dead on December 26 by a police officer in an apartment in Chicago when he was responding to a report of a domestic disturbance.

Dec. 28

According to a toll report by the website of the Gun Violence Archive, there were a total of 51,675 gun violence incidents in the United States in 2015, including 329 mass shootings. Altogether 13,136 were killed and 26,493 injured, including 682 children aged zero to 11 and 2,640 teens aged 12 to 17.

Dec. 31

According to data posted on *the Washington Post* website, 990 people were fatally shot by police in the United States in 2015. On a monthly basis, police shot dead 76 people in January, 77 in February, 92 in March, 84 in April, 71 in May, 65 in June, 104 in July, 94 in August, 80 in September, 82 in October, 76 in November and 89 in December.

2015年美国的人权纪录

中华人民共和国国务院新闻办公室

2016年4月

导言

美国国务院于当地时间4月13日发布《2015年国别人权报告》，再一次对世界各国人权状况妄加置评，而对自身存在的严重人权问题却三缄其口，毫无反思之意。2015年的美国人权，不仅旧的问题未得到解决，而且新的问题不断滋生。既然美国政府不肯拿起镜子照照自己，那么也只好由别人来帮助完成了。

关于2015年美国的人权纪录，以下事实是凿凿在册的。

——美国枪支管理失控，公民生命权受到严重威胁。枪击案件频发，是2015年美国留给世人最深刻的印象。截至2015年12月28日，当年共发生枪击事件51675起，造成13136人死亡、26493人受伤。

——美国警察暴力执法，公民人身安全无法保障。截至2015年12月24日，警察当年共射杀965人，警方滥用权力的行为并未得到应有的追究。巴尔的摩暴发了“为弗雷迪伸张正义”的抗议活动，芝加哥市民为麦克唐纳之死举行了大规模游行，明尼阿波利斯市的民众因贾马尔·克拉克被警察枪杀而包围警察局。

——美国监狱系统腐败丛生，严重侵犯囚犯人权。佛罗里达州一所监狱的狱警将患有精神疾患的囚犯达伦·莱尼在淋浴间活活烫死。美国最大的女子监狱罗维尔监狱的狱警逼迫数百名女囚卖淫以换取基本的生活物资和保护，在过去十年间已有57名囚犯死在了该监狱。

——美国金钱政治和家族政治大行其道，公民政治权利难以得到有效保障。企业和个人可以向超级政治行动委员会无限额捐款以影响美国大选，企业通过金钱影响政治并获取巨额回报。有评论认为，美国的政治体系已被颠覆为向主要政治捐助者提供回报的工具。家族出身成为美国政治中的主导因素，少数家族和幕后利益集团用资金影响选举。美国党派之争绑架民意，因为选举利益导致民主党与共和党无法协调制定真正符合民意的政策。

——美国社会问题严重，保障公民经济和社会权利困难重重。2014年有4670万人处于贫困状态。每年至少有4810万人缺乏食物保障。2015年有超过56万人无家可归。79%的美国人相信更多人会掉出而不是上升到中产阶级行列。如今，美国仍有3300万人没有医疗保险，4400万受雇于私人部门的劳动者无法享受带薪病假的权利，占私人部门劳动者总数的40%。

——美国种族矛盾尖锐，种族关系处于近20年来最差时期。61%的美国人认为美国的种族关系糟糕。执法司法领域是种族歧视的重灾区。88%的非洲裔美国人相信自己受到警察不公正对待，68%的非洲裔美国人认为刑事司法体系存在种族歧视。非洲裔美国人拥有的财富仅为白人的十二分之一，拉美裔为十一分之一。有评论认为，对于许多非洲裔和拉美裔美国家庭而言，美国梦仍然遥不可及。

——美国妇女状况不断恶化，儿童成长环境堪忧。全职女性与全职男性2014年的年薪收入比为79：100。过去十年内贫困妇女比例从12.1%上升至14.5%。国际劳工组织指出，美国是唯一没有立法明确规定妇女带薪产假的工业化国家。23%的大学本科女生遭受性骚扰或性侵犯。2015年每个月至少发生两起校园枪击案，几乎每周都有两个孩子遭受意外枪击死亡，15岁以上因伤死亡的青少年中有四分之一死于枪击事件。约1740万由单亲妈妈抚养的儿童中，45%生活在贫困线以下。约五分之一的儿童生活在食品保障不足的家庭。

——美国仍在公然粗暴侵犯他国人权，视他国生命如草芥。美国在伊拉克和叙利亚的空袭行动炸死数千平民。美国在巴基斯坦和也门肆意开展无人机袭击，造成数百平民死亡。美军2015年10月3日对阿富汗昆都士“无国界医生”组织医院野蛮空袭，42人惨遭杀害。美国政府无视国际社会的强烈谴责，仍未关闭建立14年之久的关塔那摩监狱，至今仍有近100人在被任意拘留多年且未经审判的情况下继续被羁押。

一、公民权利遭到肆意侵犯

2015年，美国枪支犯罪猖獗，警察滥用暴力，监狱腐败严重，秘密监控个人信息频现，公民权利遭到肆意侵犯。

暴力犯罪威胁公民生命和财产安全。据美国联邦调查局2015年发布的《美国犯罪报告》，2014年美国共发生暴力犯罪1165383起，平均每十万居民中发生365.5起，其中谋杀案件14249起，强奸案件84041起，抢劫案件325802起，严重暴力伤害案件741291起；共发生财产犯罪案件8277829起，平均每十万居民中发生2596.1起，被害人因财产犯罪遭受的损失超过143亿美元。(注1)英国《经济学人》网站2015年12月1日刊文分析，美国一些城市的犯罪率大幅攀升，巴尔的摩和圣路易斯2015年上半年的谋杀率分别比去年同期增长了48%和59%。(注2)美国国家帮派研究中心的詹姆斯·豪威尔指出，美国过去5年帮派数量增长8%，帮派成员数量增长11%，与帮派相关的谋杀案增加23%。(注3)

枪支泛滥造成公民生命权无法得到保障。统计显示，美国有3亿多人口，私人枪支保有量逾3亿支。过去十年里，超过400万美国人成为袭击、抢劫和其他涉枪犯罪的受害者。据美国枪支暴力档案室发布的《2015年枪支暴力伤亡统计》，截至2015年12月28日，美国当年共发生枪击事件51675起，其中大规模枪击事件329起；共造成13136人死亡、26493人受伤。(注4)美国联邦调查局2015年发布的《美国犯罪报告》显示，2014年美国发生的谋杀案件中有67.9%使用枪支，抢劫案件中有40.3%使用枪支，严重暴力袭击案中有22.5%使用枪支。(注5)

警察暴力执法严重侵犯人权。美国警方在执法过程中过度使用暴力，造成大量普通公民伤亡。据《华盛顿邮报》网站统计，截至2015年12月24日，警察当年共射杀965人。[注6]巴尔的摩25岁非洲裔男子弗雷迪·格雷因警察暴力致死，引发了“为弗雷迪伸张正义”的抗议活动。[注7]射杀17岁非洲裔男孩麦克唐纳的芝加哥警察，迟迟未被起诉，公众为此举行抗议游行。该警察之前曾遭20项投诉，未受到任何追究。[注8]美国全国广播公司2015年11月19日报道，明尼阿波利斯市24岁的非洲裔男子贾马尔·克拉克在已被警方控制的情况下被击毙，民众包围警察局抗议示威，引发暴力冲突。[注9]

政府秘密监控公民个人信息，侵犯公民隐私。据《华盛顿邮报》网站2015年12月1日报道，美国联邦调查局利用其特权强迫互联网公司未经法庭批准向其提供用户信息，包括全部的网络浏览记录。[注10]皮尤研究中心2015年5月29日发布的报告显示，大多数美国人反对政府大规模收集公民信息，有三分之二的人认为政府在收集信息方面没有足够的限制，61%的人越来越怀疑政府相关计划的目的，54%的人反对政府将收集电话和互联网信息作为反恐的手段，74%的人不同意为了安全的目的放弃隐私权和自由，93%的人认为应对收集信息的人加以管控，90%的人认为应对收集何种私人信息的种类加强管控。[注11]

狱警肆意践踏囚犯人权。据《迈阿密先驱报》网站2015年12月连续报道，美国最大的女子监狱罗维尔监狱充斥着腐败、酷刑和性虐待，狱警将数百名女囚视为妓女，逼迫她们卖淫以换取基本的生活物资、保护或奖励。在过去十年间已有57名囚犯死在了该监狱，该数字尚未包括被送往医院的囚犯。[注12]《华盛顿邮报》网站2015年5月13日报道，费尔法克斯郡一所监狱的狱警用电击枪将女性精神病患者娜塔莎·麦肯娜杀害。[注13]福克斯新闻网网站2015年4月9日报道，佛罗里达州一所监狱的狱警被控虐待和杀害囚犯，其中患有精神疾患的囚犯达伦·莱尼被强迫淋浴长达两个小时，水温高达华氏180度。他虽大声求饶呼救，却无人理睬，最后竟被活活烫死。[注14]

(注1) 美国联邦调查局报告，见www.fbi.gov。

(注2) 英国《经济学人》网站（www.economist.com），2015年12月1日。

(注3)《美国新闻与世界报道》网站（www.usnews.com），2015年3月6日。

(注4) 美国枪支暴力档案室网站（www.gunviolencearchive.org），2015年12月28日。

(注5) 美国联邦调查局报告，见www.fbi.gov。

(注6)《华盛顿邮报》网站（www.washingtonpost.com），2015年12月24日。

(注7)《今日美国》网站（www.usatoday.com），2015年12月22日。

(注8) 美国有线电视新闻网网站（edition.cnn.com），2015年11月26日。

(注9) 美国全国广播公司网站（www.nbc.com），2015年11月19日。

(注10)《华盛顿邮报》网站（www.washingtonpost.com），2015年12月1日。

(注11) 皮尤中心网站（www.pewresearch.org），2015年5月29日。

(注12)《迈阿密先驱报》网站（www.miamiherald.com），2015年12月12日、13日、16日。

(注13)《华盛顿邮报》网站（www.washingtonpost.com），2015年5月13日。

(注14) 福克斯新闻网网站（www.foxnews.com），2015年4月9日。

二、政治权利无法得到应有保障

2015年，美国金钱政治和家族政治变本加厉，选民的真实意愿难以有效表达，政治生活中存在事实上的信仰歧视，公民知情权受到进一步压制。对此，美国前总统吉米·卡特发出“美国已经不再是民主国家了”的感慨。(注15)

金钱政治暴露民主虚伪性。美国法律对个人向总统候选人捐款数额作了限制，但对个人和企业向超级政治行动委员会捐款没有限制。《今日美国》2015年4月10日报道，至少有11个总统候选人联盟成立了超级政治行动委员会，借以筹集无限额捐款支持竞选。(注16)总统候选人和超级政治行动委员会仅用半年时间，就筹集到3.8亿美元，其中60多笔100万美元以上的捐款占三分之一，一半捐款来自出资10万美元以上的捐款人，67位出资最多的捐款人捐款总额是50.8万名最小额捐助者的3倍还多。(注17)据美国财经博客网披露，2007—2012年，在政治方面最为活跃的200家企业共耗费58亿美元用于联邦游说和竞选捐款，而它们则从联邦政府项目和支持中获得4.4万亿美元的回报，占美国个人纳税者向联邦政府所缴税款的三分之二。这意味着，企业为影响美国政治的花费可以获取760倍的回报。(注18)美国前总统吉米·卡特就此指出，无限额的政治贿赂成为提名总统候选人或当选总统的主要影响因素，“美国的政治体系已被颠覆为向主要政治捐助者提供回报的工具”。(注19)美国总统2016年国情咨文也承认金钱对政治的影响很大，称“少数家族和幕后利益集团利用资金影响选举”。

家族政治左右美国选举。在参加2016年美国总统选举的候选人中，有多名参选人家族政治背景明显。《纽约时报》通过大数据分析得出结论，“父辈优势”在政治领域明显。美国总统的儿子成为总统的几率比同龄人高140万倍，州长的儿子成为州长的概率比普通美国人高6000倍，参议员子承父业的机会比普通美国男性高出8500倍。(注20) 据《华盛顿邮报》2015年1月16日报道，自从共和党建立以来，其8.7%的国会议员与前国会议员是近亲。该报道还指出，美国总统竞选充满贵族继承制的气息：有可能入围候选人名单的是州长和总统候选人的儿子、国会议员和总统候选人的儿子、总统的妻子和总统的兄弟、总统的儿子和参议员的孙子。(注21)

信仰歧视使政治生活失去公平。在美国，不信仰上帝可能成为公职竞选中的最大限制。不信仰基督教的人想赢得竞选是非常困难的，而不信仰任何宗教的人想赢得竞选则更加困难。据《华盛顿邮报》网站2015年9月22日报道，皮尤中心2014年5月的一次调查显示，无神论被视为潜在总统候选人不合格的最重要因素，超过一半的人表示他们不太可能将选票投给一个不信仰上帝的人。同年7月的另一次调查显示，在所有与宗教相关的群体中，无神论者和穆斯林被美国人予以最负面的评价。(注22)

公民选举权受到进一步限制。据《美国新闻与世界报道》网站2015年8月4日披露，2010年以来，已经有21个州通过了新的法律来限制投票权的行使，一些州缩短了提前投票时间，其他的州则限制了证明合法选民身份的有效文件的数量。有14个州将在2016年的总统大选中首次实施限制投票权行使的新措施。公民选举权成为两党恶性竞争的牺牲品，有民主党参选人指责共和党参选人“系统和故意地”阻止数以万计的美国人投票，以达到其竞选获胜的目的。[注23]《今日美国》网站2015年3月20日报道，美国2014年中期选举的投票率为20世纪40年代以来的最低。全国的平均投票率为37%，最低为印第安纳州，只有28.8%。[注24]

选民真实意愿难以得到有效表达。据《基督教科学箴言报》网站2015年12月13日分析，两党制迫使美国选民两极分化，大多数选民并非真正支持所选择的政党，而是出于对另一政党的担心和恐惧作出无奈选择。[注25]美国总统在2016年国情咨文中承认，现有划分国会选区做法的结果是“政客选择选民，而不是选民选择政客”，“党派间的积怨和猜疑未见减弱，反而变得更深”。

公民知情权遭受政府打压。据美联社2015年3月13日报道，美国政府正在削弱有关保障公民获得信息权利的法律，公民获取政府信息的系统遭受严重破坏，公民借助公共档案向政府官员问责愈加困难。[注26]美国有线电视新闻网2015年2月13日报道，记者和新闻监管机构一直抨击本届美国政府为最不透明的政府之一。因对弗格森案的抗议，至少有15名新闻记者被捕。[注27]

(注15)《赫芬顿邮报》网站（www.huffingtonpost.com），2015年8月3日。

(注16)《今日美国》网站（www.usatoday.com），2015年4月10日。

(注17)美国在线网站（www.aol.com），2015年8月1日；politico网站（www.politico.com），2015年8月1日。

(注18)美国财经博客网（www.zerohedge.com），2015年3月16日。

(注19)《赫芬顿邮报》网站（www.huffingtonpost.com），2015年8月3日。

(注20)《纽约时报》网站（www.nytimes.com），2015年3月22日。

(注21)《华盛顿邮报》网站（www.washingtonpost.com），2015年1月16日。

(注22)《华盛顿邮报》网站（www.washingtonpost.com），2015年9月22日。

(注23)《美国新闻与世界报道》网站（www.usnews.com），2015年8月4日。

(注24)《今日美国》网站（www.usatoday.com），2015年3月20日。

(注25)《基督教科学箴言报》网站（www.csmonitor.com），2015年12月13日。

(注26)美联社网站（www.ap.org），2015年3月13日。

(注27)美国有线电视新闻网网站（edition.cnn.com），2015年2月13日。

三、经济和社会权利难以有效实现

2015年，美国在经济和社会权利保障方面缺乏实质性进步，工人为维护工作权利举行大规模罢工，食物无保障者和无家可归者数量庞大，公众健康状况堪忧。

劳动者的工作权利未能得到有效保障。据半岛电视台美国频道网站2015年10月6日报道，美国4400万受雇于私人部门的劳动者无法享受带薪病假的权利，占私人部门劳动者总数的40%。很多行业出现了大规模的罢工。2015年2月，加利福尼亚、得克萨斯、肯塔基和华盛顿州9个炼油厂的工人举行罢工，抗议繁重的加班、不稳定的岗位和危险的工作环境。[注28]2015年4月，230个城市的快餐店职员罢工，以争取15美元的最低工资；11月，数百个城市的快餐店职员为此再次罢工并示威游行，全美7个主要机场的2000多名工作人员也进行了罢工以抗议过低的工资水平。[注29]

贫富差距悬殊。美国最穷的20%人口的收入仅占全民总收入的3.1%，而最富有的20%人口的收入占到51.4%。[注30]官方公布的2014年的贫困人口达到4670万人。[注31]以特拉华州为例，生活在贫困线以下的人口由2013年的11.7%上升到了12.5%，其中威尔明顿市贫困线以下的人口占到了近25%，儿童的贫困率则高达20%左右。美国民众对社会经济波动前景感到悲观，79%的人相信更多人会掉出而不是上升到中产阶级行列。[注32]

食物无保障者规模庞大。据英国《卫报》网站2015年11月26日报道，2008—2014年间，美国每年至少有4810万人被官方认定为“食物无保障者”，包括19.2%有孩子的家庭，这意味着他们的均衡饮食难以保障。[注33]据美国疾病控制与防治中心评估，每年有4800万人会患上食源性疾病，其中12.8万人需要住院治疗，3000人因此丧命。[注34]根据美国农业部的最新数据，大约五分之一的儿童生活在食品保障不足的家庭。[注35]

数十万人无家可归。《今日美国》网站2015年6月9日报道，美国近几年住房价格快速上涨，而居民收入却停滞不前，55%的民众不得不为住房付出更高代价。全美地产经纪商协会的报告指出，房租和家庭收入之间的差距已经扩大到无法维持的水平。[注36]据美国住房和城市发展部的报告，截至2015年11月18日，全国超过56万人无家可归，其中包括25%的18岁以下儿童。[注37]以纽约为例，2015年10月共有59568名无家可归者每天夜里在庇护所里度过，比2005年高出86%，其中包括14361个家庭和23858名儿童。露宿街头的无家可归者普遍面临着缺乏如厕和洗澡场所等问题。[注38]洛杉矶、西雅图、波特兰和夏威夷州近年来都曾因无家可归者增多而宣布进入紧急状态。[注39]

健康权保障不力。据美国政策创新研究所2015年9月18日发表的分析报告，尽管美国国会在2010年就通过了政府提出的医疗改革法案，承诺要建立全民医保体系，但至今仍有3300万人没有医疗保险。[注40]美国医疗护理水平在11个发达国家中排倒数第一，婴儿死亡率最高。[注41]全国有超过6200个地方缺乏初级护理医生。[注42]全国艾滋病感染者超过120万人，其中八分之一的感染者并不知情。[注43]贫富群体的健康保障存在显著差异。据法新社2015年10月14日报道，纽约市布鲁克林区布朗斯维尔街区近40%的人生活在贫困线以下，其居民新感染艾滋病毒的比率为全纽约市的2倍多，人均寿命比曼哈顿金融区的居民少11年。[注44]

药物滥用致死率再创新高。据美国疾病控制与防治中心报告显示，药物滥用成为当前美国主要的致病原因。药物滥用致死率1999年至2013年增长了1倍多，从每十万居民6.0人上升至13.8人。2014年，因药物滥用造成超过47000人死亡，比2013年增加3018人。在所有药物滥用中，海洛因滥用尤为突出。2002年至2013年，海洛因过量使用致死人数翻了近两番，达到8200多人，2014年又猛增至10574人。在海洛因吸食者中，青年和女性增长明显。与2002年至

2004年相比，2011年至2013年吸食海洛因的18至25岁青年人数增长了109%，女性增长了100%。(注45)

(注28) 半岛电视台美国频道网站（america.aljazeera.com），2015年2月2日、10月6日。

(注29)《思考进步》网站（thinkprogress.org），2015年4月15日；《今日美国》网站（www.usatoday.com），2015年11月10日、19日。

(注30)《今日美国》网站（www.usatoday.com），2015年10月10日。

(注31) 美国人口普查局报告，见www.census.gov。

(注32)《今日美国》网站（www.usatoday.com），2015年6月9日、11月23日。

(注33) 英国《卫报》网站（www.theguardian.com），2015年11月26日。

(注34) 皮尤慈善信托组织网站（www.pewtrusts.org），2015年12月4日。

(注35) 半岛电视台美国频道网站（america.aljazeera.com），2015年10月8日。

(注36)《今日美国》网站（www.usatoday.com），2015年6月9日、7月31日。

(注37) 美国住房和城市发展部的报告，见www.hud.gov。

(注38) 皮尤慈善信托组织网站（www.pewtrusts.org），2015年11月11日。

(注39) 伊朗PRESS TV网站（www.presstv.ir），2015年11月20日。

(注40) 美国政策创新研究所网站（www.ipi.org），2015年9月18日。

(注41) 博根项目网站（borgenproject.org），2015年8月23日。

(注42)《华盛顿邮报》网站（www.washingtonpost.com），2015年12月12日。

(注43) 美国有线电视新闻网网站（edition.cnn.com），2015年12月9日。

(注44) 法新社，2015年10月14日。

(注45) 美国疾病防控中心网站（www.cdc.gov），2015年10月16日、12月29日；《美国新闻与世界报道》网站（www.usnews.com），2015年12月18日。

四、种族歧视变本加厉

2015年，美国的种族关系持续恶化，执法司法领域依然是种族歧视的重灾区，种族仇恨犯罪时有发生，反穆斯林言论甚嚣尘上，少数族裔在经济和社会生活中的弱势地位难以扭转。

种族关系为近20年来最糟糕年份。美国哥伦比亚广播公司与《纽约时报》2015年5月4日联合发布的调查显示，61%的美国人认为美国的种族关系差，这是1992年以来的最高点，大多数非洲裔和白人美国人均认为美国种族关系处于糟糕状态。(注46)《华尔街日报》和美国全国广播公司新闻网2015年12月的联合调查显示，认为美国的种族关系处于良好状态的美国人从2009年1月的77%下降到34%。(注47)美国公共宗教研究所2015年11月发布的调查结果显示，35%的被调查者认为自己居住的社区存在种族紧张问题，比2012年增长了18个百分点。(注48)皮尤中心2015年8月发布的数据显示，50%的美国人认为种族主义是美国社会的严重问题；60%的美国人认为国家需要继续努力促进种族平等，比一年前高出14个百分点。(注49)

警察杀害非洲裔美国人的案件屡屡发生。2015年11月15日，明尼苏达州明尼阿波利斯市24岁非洲裔男子贾马尔·克拉克被白人警察开枪打死。事发时，两名警察正试图逮捕他。据目击者称，克拉克头部中枪时双手戴着手铐。一个名为“黑人生命很重要”的民权团体在全国多个城市组织抗议游行。活动组织者在社交网站上表示，

“现在整个美国都弥漫着反对有色人种的白人至上恐怖主义。”(注50) 2015年4月12日，25岁的非洲裔男子弗雷迪·格雷在马里兰州西巴尔的摩地区遭警方逮捕时，被警察用膝盖顶住背部和头部、双手反铐在背后、脸朝下拖进警车。在发现格雷呼吸困难并要求帮助后，警察并未理会。格雷随后出现昏迷，直至送医院后死亡，死因是脊柱严重受伤。事件引发巴尔的摩市居民大规模抗议示威。示威活动27日演变成暴力冲突，导致马里兰州宣布进入紧急状态，并出动国民警卫队维持秩序。这是继2014年白人警察枪杀非洲裔少年布朗引发弗格森骚乱后，美国州政府6个月内第二次动用国民警卫队维护秩序。《纽约时报》4月28日评论称，“格雷成为这个国家警察暴行的最新象征。”(注51) 据《华盛顿邮报》网站统计，截至2015年12月24日，警察全年共射杀965人，其中36人是手无寸铁的非洲裔美国人。(注52)美国哥伦比亚广播公司与《纽约时报》2015年5月4日联合发布的调查显示，79%的非洲裔美国人认为警察更容易针对非洲裔使用致命性武器，非洲裔比白人更倾向于认为地方警察带给他们的是焦虑感而不是安全感。(注53)全美律师协会公布的一项调查显示，88%的非洲裔和59%的白人相信非洲裔美国人遭受到警察不公正的对待。(注54)

刑事司法领域种族歧视严重。2015年盖勒普公司的一项调查显示，68%的非洲裔美国人和37%的白人认为美国的刑事司法体系存在种族歧视。(注55)公共宗教研究所的调查显示，51%的美国人认为非洲裔和其他少数族裔在刑事司法体系中与白人相比受到了不平等对待，78%的非洲裔美国人认为他们在刑事司法体系中受到不平等待遇。(注56)在一些案件审判过程中，公诉人在选任陪审团成员时会刻意将符合条件的非洲裔陪审员排除出去。在美国南部地区，这种操纵陪审团种族构成的做法极为常见。(注57)

种族仇恨犯罪时有发生。46岁的克雷格·斯蒂芬·希克斯于2015年2月10日在北卡罗莱纳大学附近枪杀三名穆斯林学生，凶手此前时常在网络上发表各种反宗教言论。(注58)21岁的白人男子戴伦·鲁夫2015年6月17日晚在南卡罗莱纳州查尔斯顿一个非洲裔美国人教堂内枪杀了包括牧师在内的9人。鲁夫在行凶时对受害者大喊："你们强奸我们的妇女，占领我们的国家，你们必须滚出去。"(注59)

反穆斯林言论甚嚣尘上。英国《卫报》网站2015年11月19日报道，一位共和党总统参选人公开发表言论，称会考虑对穆斯林实施未经授权的搜查，增加对清真寺的监控，并声称不排除建立追踪美国穆斯林的数据库，或给穆斯林颁发标明其宗教信仰的特殊身份证。(注60)12月7日，该参选人又声称"应全面禁止穆斯林进入美国"。(注61)近年来，美国人对伊斯兰教的看法变得越来越负面。美国公共宗教研究所的调查发现，56%的美国民众认为伊斯兰教与美国基本价值相冲突，持此观点的共和党人高达76%。(注62)联合国人权委员会对美国"执法人员对某些族裔群体特别是穆斯林的监视表示关切"。(注63)

少数族裔处境艰难。美国劳工统计局数据显示，2015年11月白人失业率为4.3%，非洲裔为9.4%，拉美裔为6.4%。非洲裔失业率是白人失业率的两倍以上，拉美裔失业率比白人高出近50%。(注64)非洲裔大学生失业率与白人高中生失业率大致相当。(注65)在爱荷华州，33%的非洲裔家庭年收入低于2万美元，而只有8%的白人家庭低于此数。超过20%的白人家庭年收入超过10万美元，而只有8%的非洲裔家庭能达到同样水平。(注66)在纽约无家可归者收容所的受助者中，约57%是非洲裔，31%是拉美裔，8%是白人。(注67)据美国有线电视新闻网网站2015年2月18日报道，种族之间的收入不平等进一步扩大，白人拥有的财富是非洲裔的12倍，是拉美裔的近11倍，“对于很多非洲裔和拉美裔美国家庭而言，美国梦仍然遥不可及”。(注68)非洲裔美国人达内尔·沃克拍摄的纪录片《寻求避难》在互联网上放映后，引起强烈反响。该片记录了非洲裔美国人的困境。由于警察的野蛮执法等原因，一些非洲裔美国人在美国不再感到安全，希望转到其他地方定居。针对美国连续发生的警察杀害非洲裔事件，2004年从美国移居法国的作家迈尔斯·马歇尔·刘易斯在2014年出版了《黑人没有国家》一书。(注69)

(注46) 美国哥伦比亚广播公司纽约分支机构网站（newyork.cbslocal.com），2015年5月4日。

(注47)《华尔街日报》博客网（blogs.wsj.com），2015年12月16日。

(注48) 美国公共宗教研究所网站（publicreligion.org），2015年11月17日。

(注49) people-press 网站（www.people-press.org），2015年8月5日；《华盛顿邮报》网站（www.washingtonpost.com），2015年8月5日。

(注50) 美国《大西洋》月刊网站（www.theatlantic.com），2015年11月18日；明尼苏达州公共广播电台新闻网站（www.mprnews.org），2015年11月20日；《赫芬顿邮报》网站（www.huffingtonpost.com），2015年11月24日。

(注51) 美国有线电视新闻网网站（edition.cnn.com），2015年4月29日；英国广播公司网站（www.bbc.com），2015年5月5日；美国哥伦比亚广播公司巴尔的摩分支机构网站（baltimore.cbslocal.com），2015年4月27日；《纽约时报》网站（www.nytimes.com），2015年4月27日、28日。

(注52)《华盛顿邮报》网站（www.washingtonpost.com），2015年12月24日。

(注53) 美国哥伦比亚广播公司纽约分支机构网站（newyork.cbslocal.com），2015年5月4日。

(注54)《今日美国》网站（www.usatoday.com），2015年9月9日。

(注55)《今日美国》网站（www.usatoday.com），2015年6月18日。

(注56) 美国公共宗教研究所网站（publicreligion.org），2015年5月7日。

(注57)《纽约客》网站（www.newyorker.com），2015年6月5日。

(注58) 印度《印度快报》网站（indianexpress.com），2015年6月5日。

(注59) 美国哥伦比亚广播公司网站（www.cbsnews.com），2015年6月17日；英国广播公司网站（www.bbc.com），2015年6月19日。

(注60) 英国《卫报》网站（www.theguardian.com），2015年11月19日。

(注61)英国《经济学人》网站（www.economist.com），2015年12月8日。

(注62)《华盛顿邮报》网站（www.washingtonpost.com），2015年11月17日。

(注63) 联合国报告A/70/255，见daccess-dds-ny.un.org。

(注64) 美国劳工统计局2015年12月4日报告，见www.bls.gov。

(注65)《赫芬顿邮报》网站（huffingtonpost.com），2015年12月18日。

(注66)《今日美国》网站（www.usatoday.com），2015年10月31日。

(注67) 无家可归者联盟网站（www.coalitionforthehomeless.org），

2015年3月18日。

(注68) 美国有线电视新闻网网站（money.cnn.com），2015年2月18日。

(注69) thedailybeast网站（www.thedailybeast.com），2015年11月11日。

五、妇女和儿童权利堪忧

2015年，美国妇女和儿童权利受到严重侵犯。妇女遭受职场歧视、家庭暴力和性侵犯的情况严重，儿童面临枪支、虐待、贫困和警察暴力的威胁。

女性社会地位下降。2015年12月11日，联合国“在法律和实践中歧视妇女问题工作组”实地考察后指出，美国仍然没有落实普遍带薪产假、生育保健和政治选举中的平等机会等权利和保护措施。美国妇女在公共和政治领域的任职率、经济与社会权利保障、健康和安全保护等方面低于国际标准。女性在各州立法机构中所占席位平均值为24.9%，在全球仅排第72位。两性之间的收入差距为21%；过去十年，贫困妇女比例从12.1%上升至14.5%，该数字高于男性。贫困妇女、移徙妇女在获取性健康和生殖健康服务方面面临更大的障碍。缺乏枪支管制给妇女安全造成很大威胁，在一些家庭暴力案件中尤其严重，被拘留妇女和美洲原住民妇女遭受暴力的比例很高。(注70)

女性面临职场歧视。美国人口普查局2015年9月发布的数据显示，2014年全职女性比全职男性的平均年薪少10762美元，二者的平均年薪收入比为79：100。(注71)国际劳工组织根据2014年185个国家和地区的可用数据指出，美国是唯一没有立法明确规定带薪产假的工业化国家。[注72]《洛杉矶时报》网站2015年5月6日报道，在美国高科技企业2013年的晋升过程中，白人男性比白人女性拥有42%的优势，相对亚裔女性的优势则高达260%。[注73]

女性遭受不同形式的性骚扰和性侵犯。美国高等院校联合会2015年9月发布的调查结果显示，23%的大学本科女生遭受过性骚扰或性侵犯，20%的大学生认为性侵犯和不当性行为成为大学校园中极为严重的问题。[注74]据《今日美国》网站2015年8月17日报道，37%的美国女性曾遭受网络性骚扰，而拉美裔和非洲裔妇女遭受性骚扰的比例分别高达54%、51%。许多网络性骚扰发展为现实生活中的跟踪和性骚扰。[注75]据《今日美国》网站2015年12月11日报道，俄克拉荷马州前警官丹尼尔·霍尔茨克劳被控在自己巡逻的低收入社区中性侵女性。在他被判已经证实的18项罪名中，涉及的8名受害者均为非洲裔女性。[注76]

枪支威胁儿童安全。据美国枪支暴力档案室网站发布的《2015年枪支暴力伤亡统计》，截至12月28日，美国2015年发生的枪击案件导致682名11岁以下的儿童伤亡，2640名12岁至17岁的青少年伤亡。[注77]据俄罗斯电视台网站2015年10月10日报道，当年美国已发生52起校园枪击案，每个月至少发生2起。[注78]据《今日美国》网站2015年1月22日报道，美国几乎每周都有两名儿童遭受意外枪击死亡，近三分之二的意外死亡发生在受害者的家里或者车中。[注79]根据美国儿科学会的调查，美国15岁以上因伤致死的青少年中，有四分之一死于枪击事件。[注80]

儿童健康和生活状况不佳。美国疾病和预防中心的统计显示，新生儿患有梅毒的比率在2012—2014年间增长了38%，是2001年以来的最高水平。[注81]美国正在接受治疗的吸毒者中，有五分之一是18岁之前通过父母初次接触毒品的。[注82]美国人口普查局的调查显示，2015年约有1740万儿童由单亲妈妈抚养，其中45%生活在贫困线以下。[注83]在纽约，近6%的非洲裔儿童和近3%的拉美裔儿童因无家可归需要求助于庇护所。[注84]《今日美国》网站2015年8月15日报道，47%的农村拉美裔婴儿和41%的城市拉美裔婴儿出生于贫困家庭。农村地区的婴儿很难享受到诸如联邦和州为妇女儿童提供的特殊营养项目，陷于贫困的可能性更大，“这些孩子一出生就输在了人生的起跑线上”。[注85]

儿童遭遇虐待。《华盛顿邮报》网站2015年1月1日报道，发生在华盛顿及周边地区的多数儿童死亡案件的作案人是家长或其他监护人。[注86]《迈阿密先驱报》网站2015年3月10日报道，在佛罗里达州，三分之一的女孩和五分之一的男孩在18岁前可能遭受性侵害。这些受虐经历会对受害者未来的生活造成严重的负面影响，平均每位受虐者会因为受害经历在其一生中失去250000美元的收入，一半的受害者在校学习成绩低于平均成绩。[注87]

非洲裔儿童成为警察暴力的受害者。美国有线电视新闻网财经频道网站2015年6月10日报道，得克萨斯州麦金利警察局的白人警察暴力对待一名14岁非洲裔女孩的视频在网上广泛传播。该警察在处置一起来自泳池聚会的报警时，大声辱骂几个非洲裔青少年，并将身穿泳衣的非洲裔女孩猛烈摔到地面，后来甚至拔出配枪对准他们。现场拍摄视频的白人目击者认为该警察的行为毫无疑问是出于种族主义动机。这一事件引发民众的抗议游行。[注88] 2015年10月26日，南卡罗莱纳州春谷高中的驻校白人警察本·菲尔茨对一名非洲裔女生施暴的视频在网上引发民众愤慨。该校警猛掐这名在课堂上玩手机的女孩的颈部，将其连人带椅狠狠摔倒在地，最后拖出教室。菲尔茨2013年曾因不公平且粗暴对待非洲裔学生被告上法庭。美国全国有色人种协进会称，从未有白人学生遭受如此暴力对待。美国公民自由联盟南卡罗莱纳州分支机构主管维多利亚·米德尔顿认为，无论出于何种目的，在课堂上对年轻孩子过度使用暴力的行为都无法容忍，“学校不应该成为孩子们被粗暴对待的地方”。[注89]

(注70) 联合国人权高专办网站（www.ohchr.org），2015年12月11日。

(注71) 美国人口普查局报告，见www.census.gov。

(注72) 美国广播公司新闻网站（abcnews.go.com），2015年5月6日。

(注73)《洛杉矶时报》网站（www.latimes.com），2015年5月6日。

(注74)《洛杉矶时报》网站（www.latimes.com），2015年9月21日；《华盛顿邮报》网站（www.washingtonpost.com），2015年9月1日、21日。

(注75)《今日美国》网站（www.usatoday.com），2015年8月17日。

(注76)《今日美国》网站（www.usatoday.com），2015年12月11日。

(注77) 美国枪支暴力档案室网站（www.gunviolencearchive.org），2015年12月28日。

(注78) 俄罗斯电视台网站（www.rt.com），2015年10月10日。

(注79)《今日美国》网站（www.usatoday.com），2015年1月22日。

(注80) 美国《大西洋》月刊网站（www.theatlantic.com），2015年1月12日。

(注81)《华盛顿邮报》网站（www.washingtonpost.com），2015年11月12日。

(注82) 美国广播公司新闻网站（abcnews.go.com），2015年8月24日。

(注83) singlemotherguide网站（singlemotherguide.com），2015年6月1日。

(注84) 无家可归者联盟网站（www.coalitionforthehomeless.org），2015年3月19日。

(注85)《今日美国》网站（www.usatoday.com），2015年8月15日。

(注86)《华盛顿邮报》网站（www.washingtonpost.com），2015年1月1日。

(注87)《迈阿密先驱报》网站（www.miamiherald.com），2015年3月10日。

(注88) 美国有线电视新闻网财经频道网站（edition.cnn.com），2015年6月10日。

(注89) 美国广播公司新闻网站（abcnews.go.com），2015年10月28日。

六、粗暴侵犯他国人权

2015年，美国依然变本加厉侵犯他国人权，造成大量平民伤亡，海外监听项目侵犯公民隐私权，关塔那摩监狱的虐囚丑闻仍在继续。美国迄今未批准联合国多项核心人权公约，并对联合国重要人权决议投反对票。

空袭行动造成大量平民伤亡。据空中战争跟踪组织统计，2014年8月8日以来，美国不断组织联军对伊拉克和叙利亚境内武装进行空袭。截至2015年12月6日，美国空袭伊拉克3965次，空袭叙利亚2823次，据估算共造成两国境内

1695至2239名平民死亡。[注90]叙利亚政府认为美国主导的空袭行动是赤裸裸的“侵略行为”。[注91]2015年10月3日，阿富汗昆都士的“无国界医生”组织医院受到美军持续近半小时的空袭，许多无法行动的病人在病床上被当场炸死，一些逃出医院的医护人员遭到空中扫射，共造成42人遇难，许多尸体难以辨认。[注92]

频繁使用无人机滥杀无辜。英国《每日邮报》网站2015年10月15日报道，美国军队在执行无人机暗杀计划时仅仅使用追踪电话数据这一有限的方式来确定袭击目标。2012年1月至2013年2月美军在阿富汗东北部发动的一场代号为“干草机”的行动中，219人被炸死，其中仅有35人是预先要攻击的目标。在另一次长达5个月的行动中，90%被杀死的人都不是预先要攻击的目标，但是所有死者都被贴上了“阵亡敌人”的标签。[注93]《华盛顿邮报》网站2015年4月24日报道，根据一份研究报告，2001年“9 · 11”事件以来，美国在巴基斯坦和也门进行的415次无人机袭击中，估算造成423至962名平民死亡。[注94]美国滥用无人机袭击的做法，不仅受到国际社会的广泛批评，也被美国学术界强烈质疑。2015年3月20日，《华盛顿邮报》网站专门介绍了安德鲁 · 科伯恩所著的《杀人链条：高科技暗杀的兴起》和格里高利 · 查马尤所著的《无人机原理》两本书。安德鲁 · 科伯恩认为，“美国在全球部署具有毁灭性军事力量的过程中，无人机轰炸政策是其中一种充满着谎言、欺骗和贪婪的历史模式的顶点，是此前美国暗杀政策的延续。无人机轰炸政策不但没有实现加强美国国家安全的目标，而且还削弱了民主的进程，并在被空袭国制造了混乱，成为滋生极端主义的温床”。查马尤和科伯恩强调，无人机轰炸是一种“非人道的战争方式”，“用无人机作战，没有胜利者，只有屠杀”。[注95]

滥用酷刑践踏人权。美国参议院情报委员会公布的中情局虐囚报告指出，中情局使用的水刑、长期单独囚禁、将囚犯头部猛力撞墙和抽打乃至死亡威胁等审讯手段大大超出了法律所允许的范围。[注96]而根据有关嫌疑人的说法，美国的虐囚行为远远超出了报告所披露的内容。英国《卫报》网站2015年6月2日报道，曾被关押在关塔那摩监狱的囚犯马吉德·可汗说，审讯官将冰水倒在他的生殖器上，两次对其裸体进行录像，并不停地触摸他的“私处”；他的双脚和小腿都被放置于形如高筒靴的金属铐中，这种金属铐戳入他的肉中，使他的双腿难以动弹；狱警将他赤身裸体悬挂在木梁上长达三天，期间只提供少量饮用水而没有任何食物——他所遭受的这些酷刑都没有被写入参议院报告。[注97] 2016年1月11日，包括联合国酷刑问题特别报告员门德斯、在反恐中促进和保护人权问题特别报告员埃默森、法官和律师独立性问题特别报告员平托、任意拘留问题工作组主席洪晟弼以及欧安组织民主机构与人权办公室主任林克在内的人权专家共同发表公开信，敦促美国政府尽早关闭关塔那摩监狱。关塔那摩监狱已经建立14年之久，截至2016年1月11日，仍有近100人在被任意拘留多年且未经审判的情况下被继续羁押。[注98]

对他国政要实施监听。英国广播公司网站2015年4月

30日披露，美国国家安全局长期监听欧洲国家领导人。(注99)英国《独立报》2015年6月24日报道，美国先后对三位法国总统和其他政府高官进行了长期的电话监听，对此法国政府发言人表示“无法接受”。(注100)尽管受到来自盟国的批评，美国政府依然以国家安全为由决定对部分国家领导人实施监听。(注101)

美国口口声声标榜“人权”，以“人权卫士”自居，但时至今日，美国仍不批准《经济、社会和文化权利国际公约》《消除对妇女一切形式歧视公约》《儿童权利公约》《残疾人权利公约》等联合国核心人权公约。美国是当今世界唯一没有批准《儿童权利公约》的国家。对于国际人权事务，美国也经常采取不合作态度。对于联合国人权理事会特别机制以及联合国人权事务高级专员等对美国人权状况提出的批评，美国政府经常予以拖延或置若罔闻。2015年9月28日联合国人权理事会通过有关发展权的决议时，美国一如既往地投了反对票。(注102)

(注90) 空中战争跟踪组织网站（airwars.org）。

(注91) 英国《独立报》网站（www.independent.co.uk），2015年12月7日。

(注92) Sputnik news网站（sputniknews.com），2015年12月12日；美国广播公司新闻网站（abcnews.go.com），2015年10月5日。

(注93) 英国《每日邮报》网站（www.dailymail.co.uk），2015年10月15日。

(注94)《华盛顿邮报》网站（www.washingtonpost.com），2015年4月24日。

(注95)《华盛顿邮报》网站（www.washingtonpost.com），2015年3月

20日。

(注96) 美国参议院情报委员会报告，见www.intelligence.senate.gov。

(注97) 英国《卫报》网站（www.theguardian.com），2015年6月2日。

(注98) 联合国新闻网（www.un.org），2016年1月11日。

(注99) 英国广播公司网站（www.bbc.com），2015年4月30日。

(注100) 英国《独立报》网站（www.independent.co.uk），2015年6月24日。

(注101) 英国《卫报》网站（www.theguardian.com），2015年12月30日。

(注102) 联合国网站（www.un.org），联合国文件A/HRC/30/L.12。

附录：2015年美国侵犯人权事记

一月

3日 《华盛顿邮报》网站报道，23岁的拉美裔男子约翰·保罗·金特罗在堪萨斯州威奇托市被警察射杀。

6日 《华盛顿邮报》网站报道，34岁的女子奥特姆·斯蒂尔在爱荷华州伯灵顿被警察射杀。

同日，《华盛顿邮报》网站报道，47岁的非洲裔男子莱斯利·赛普三世在宾夕法尼亚州诺克斯维尔被警察射杀。

8日 《华盛顿邮报》网站报道，36岁的非洲裔男子阿塔戈·达蒙·霍华德在阿肯色州一个停车场内被警察射杀。

12日 美国《大西洋》月刊网站报道，根据美国儿科学会的调查，美国15岁以上因伤死亡的青少年中，有四分之一是在涉枪事件中被杀害的。

13日 《华盛顿邮报》网站报道，患有精神疾病的43岁男子理查德·麦克伦登在得克萨斯州乔丹顿他母亲的家中被警察射杀。

14日 《华盛顿邮报》网站报道，75岁的塔尔博特·施罗德因拒绝执行警察多次要求其放下手持刀具的命令，在新泽西州古桥的一所房屋内被警察射杀。

16日 《华盛顿邮报》网站发表《2016年美国总统大选了无新意》一文，指出入围候选人名单的是州长和总统候选人的儿子、国会议员和总统候选人的儿子、总统的妻子和总统的兄弟、总统的儿子和参议员的孙子，出身和名望在政治中压倒一切。

22日 《赫芬顿邮报》《今日美国》网站报道，美国弗吉尼亚州10名离职员工向法院起诉麦当劳餐厅对员工种族歧视和性骚扰，并诉称“不时遭受餐厅最高层主管的种族歧视”。因为管理者认为“有太多的黑人在该店工作”，他们在2014年遭无端解雇，工作岗位主要被白人员工替代。

29日 《华盛顿邮报》网站报道，因对警察做了一个威胁性的手势，42岁的拉尔夫·威利斯在俄克拉荷马州斯蒂尔沃特被警察射杀。

31日　《华盛顿邮报》网站报道，患有精神疾病的54岁非洲裔男子爱德华·唐纳·布莱特在马里兰州巴尔的摩一个便利店外被警察射杀。

二月

1日　半岛电视台美国频道网站报道，因为繁重的加班、不稳定的岗位和企业持续忽视危险的工作环境，来自位于加利福尼亚、得克萨斯、肯塔基和华盛顿州的9个工厂的大约3800名炼油工人于当日开始罢工。罢工组织的领导者称，这些企业每天都可能发生火灾、排放泄漏以及爆炸，威胁到当地的社区，而企业并没有采取任何措施。

2日　《华盛顿邮报》网站报道，59岁的大卫·卡希克在宾夕法尼亚州哈摩尔斯被警察用泰瑟枪击晕倒地后，又被警察在背后连开两枪打死。

同日，总部设在英国伦敦的新闻调查社发布调查报告称，2009年以来已经有至少2464人死于美国在未宣战地区的无人机轰炸。现任美国总统任内，美国对巴基斯坦、也门和索马里的无人机轰炸次数是其前任的近9倍。

4日　《华盛顿邮报》网站报道，28岁的非洲裔男子杰里米·莱特在佛罗里达州塔拉哈西市被警察连开5枪打死。

8日　《华盛顿邮报》网站报道，在2015年格莱美颁奖仪式上，美国现任总统发表视频讲话称：“美国每5个妇女中就有1个是强奸或强奸未遂的受害者。”

10日　《华盛顿邮报》网站报道，因向警车投掷石块，患有精神疾病的35岁拉美裔男子安东尼奥·桑布拉诺－蒙特斯在华盛顿帕斯科一条街道上被3个警察射杀。

同日，平等司法倡议组织发布关于美国使用私刑的研究报告，记录了1877年至1950年间3959起针对非洲裔美国人的种族恐怖私刑。报告称对非洲裔美国人的恐怖私刑增强了种族隔离。该组织负责人指出，几十年的恐怖私刑造成的地理、政治、经济和社会后果，在今天仍然可以在许多社区看到。

12日　《芝加哥论坛报》报道，过去25年来，伊利诺伊州库克郡法院有100多件明显误判案。1985年，该州男子阿博纳瑟因涉嫌强奸并杀害一名女性被捕。在警方连续审问40小时后，他在缺乏有力旁证的情况下被迫认罪并被判处终身监禁。2015年2月，DNA技术检测最终证明阿博纳瑟系无辜入狱。

13日　美国有线电视新闻网网站报道，自2009年以来，美国的新闻自由状况不断恶化。记者和新闻监管机构一直在不断地抨击现任政府是最不透明的政府之一，并顽固地试图阻碍政府信息公开。至少有15名新闻记者因对弗格森事件的抗议被捕。

同日，《华盛顿邮报》网站报道，35岁的西班牙裔男子理查德·卡林在宾夕法尼亚州一所房屋内被警察射杀。

15日　因未按警察命令放下手中所持的扫帚柄，患有精神分裂症的25岁非洲裔男子拉瓦尔·霍尔在佛罗里达州迈阿密花园街的家中被警察射杀。

18日　美国有线电视新闻网财经频道网站报道，一份新的研究报告显示，美国白人现在拥有的财富是非洲裔的12倍，是拉美裔的近11倍。在25岁至55岁年龄段中，约42%的非洲裔背负大学贷款负担，而白人却只有28%的人有大学贷款负担。“对于许多非洲裔和拉美裔家庭而言，美国梦仍然遥不可及”。

20日　《华盛顿邮报》网站报道，31岁的拉美裔男子鲁本·比利亚尔潘多在得克萨斯州尤利斯的一条街道双手举起走向警车时，被警察射杀。

27日　《华盛顿邮报》网站报道，27岁的拉美裔男子埃内斯托·贾瓦尔·卡内帕·迪亚兹在加利福尼亚州圣安娜被警察射杀在车内。

28日　《华盛顿邮报》网站报道，17岁的戴文·吉尔福德在密歇根州一个街道上与警察发生争执，被警察连开7枪打死。

同日，《华盛顿邮报》网站报道，34岁的非洲裔男子托马斯·

艾伦在密苏里州圣路易斯与警察发生口角，被警察射杀。

三月

1日　《华盛顿邮报》网站报道，因与巡警发生口角，流浪街头的13岁非洲裔男子查理·伦杜·肯昂在洛杉矶贫民窟的街头被警察射杀。

4日　《今日美国》网站连续报道，美国司法部的一项审查发现，密苏里州弗格森警察局在执法中广泛存在种族偏见，包括对非洲裔嫌犯不合理地使用武力等贯穿于整个城市的司法体系。在弗格森警察局记录的使用武力的案件中，有88%针对的是非洲裔美国人。对161个此类案件的审查发现，未有一起案件引发过纪律处分。

6日　《美国新闻与世界报道》网站报道，国家帮派研究中心研究人员指出，过去5年美国的帮派数量增长了8%，帮派成员增长了11%，与帮派相关的谋杀案增长了23%。

13日　美联社报道，利用公共档案来保持对政府官员的问责变得愈发困难和昂贵。政府正在破坏有关保障公民知情权的法律的执行，使知情权变为“不行”。

16日　美国财经博客网发表《最好的“民主”金钱可以购买》一文称，2007年至2012年，美国在政治方面最为活跃的200家企业共耗费58亿美元用于联邦游说和竞选捐款，得到4.4万亿美元的回报。

同日，《今日美国》网站报道，美国在执行信息自由法律方面处于落后位置。尽管法律规定得很好，但公共记录审计显示，在一些重要部门获取信息实际非常困难。

19日　《华盛顿邮报》网站报道，18岁的非洲裔男子布兰登·琼斯在俄亥俄州克里夫兰市闯入一家杂货店，当他从店内跑出来时被警察射杀。

20日　《今日美国》网站报道，2014年美国中期选举的投票率创20世纪40年代以来的最低。整个美国的平均投票率仅为37%，最低的印第安纳州仅为28.8%。只有7个州有超过半数的选民参与了投票。

同日，《华盛顿邮报》网站报道，自“9·11”事件以来，美国超过500次空袭行动已杀死近4000人。无人机操作者一直难以区分妇女儿童和他们所寻找的具有重要价值的目标。

26日 《时代周刊》网站报道，英国广播公司的调查显示，美国每年有成千上万的儿童遭受性剥削。许多美国儿童被卖从事性交易。贫穷和被忽视是儿童成为性交易的弱势群体的主要原因。

四月

2日 《华盛顿邮报》网站报道，44岁的非洲裔男子埃里克·哈里斯在俄克拉荷马州塔尔萨市一个街道被警察误扣扳机射杀。

8日 《今日美国》网站报道，早在“9·11”事件之前十年，美国政府便已开始秘密记录美国公民的国际通话信息，收集了数以亿计的通话记录。

9日 福克斯新闻网报道，患有精神疾病的50岁囚犯达伦·莱尼被罚在华氏180度的水中淋浴近2个小时，看守人员甚至嘲笑问他是否喜欢这样的淋浴。最终他被活活烫死。

12日 25岁的非洲裔美国人弗雷迪·格雷4月12日在巴尔的摩被拘留，其后因警察的不当行为导致死亡，在当地引发“为弗雷迪伸张正义”的大规模抗议。当局实施宵禁，国民警卫队进入该市。

15日 路透社报道，非洲裔美国人沃尔特·斯科特4月4日在手无寸铁的情况下被南卡罗莱纳州北查尔斯顿的一名白人警察射杀。上月，手无寸铁的非洲裔少年小托尼·罗宾逊在威斯康星州被一名白人警察枪杀，在数个美国城市引发游行示威，抗议警察针对少数族裔使用致命武器。

同日，《思考进步》网站报道，美国230个城市的快餐店店员4月15日离开工作岗位，进行有史以来最大规模的罢工运动，以争取15美元最低工资和建立工会的权利。

21日 《华盛顿邮报》网站报道，华盛顿雷克伍德地区37岁的丹尼尔·科瓦鲁比亚斯被警察射杀。

25日　《华盛顿邮报》网站报道，24岁的非洲裔男子大卫·费利克斯在纽约的一个公寓楼内被警察射杀。

五月

4日　哥伦比亚广播公司和《纽约时报》当日联合发布的调查显示，61%的美国人认为美国的种族关系差，这是1992年以来的最高点。

5日　《华盛顿邮报》网站报道，流浪街头的29岁非洲裔男子布兰顿·格伦在加利福尼亚州威尼斯一间酒吧外被警察射杀。

6日　美国广播公司新闻网报道，根据国际劳工组织发布的数据，美国是世界上仅有的3个不提供带薪休产假的国家之一。

7日　美国公共宗教研究所公布的调查显示，51%的美国人认为非洲裔和其他少数族裔在刑事司法体系中与白人相比受到了不平等对待，78%的非洲裔美国人认为他们在刑事司法体系中受到不平等待遇。

11日　美国5月11日接受联合国人权理事会第二次普遍定期审查。在审查期间提出的关于美国实施酷刑、继续使用死刑以及许多领域存在更多不足的报告，与美国所强调的人权改善形成鲜明对照。许多国家批评指出，在联合国已经建立的9个核心人权公约中，有6个还没有被美国批准。美国认为自己是人权的全球领导者，却没有对国际人权条约中所列出的经济、社会、文化权利作出保障。

13日　《华盛顿邮报》网站报道，患有精神疾病的女囚犯娜塔莎·麦肯娜3个月前在美国费尔法克斯郡监狱被看守人员用泰瑟电击枪4次电击致死，当时她的手和脚都已经被铁链锁住。

19日　《华盛顿邮报》网站报道，54岁的拉美裔男子阿尔弗雷多·里亚尔托雷斯在弗吉尼亚州阿灵顿的一个公寓内被警察射杀。

22日　美国有线电视新闻网网站报道，一个由60多个亚裔美国人团体组成的联盟向美国教育部和司法部提出申诉，指控哈佛大学不公平地采用更高的标准来录取亚裔美国申请人。

26日　英国广播公司网站报道，一个名为“警察暴力地图”的研究项目调查发现，在美国非洲裔被警察射杀的可能性是白人的3倍。

28日　《纽约时报》报道，最新发布的一份报告显示，种族居住隔离是“一种美国方式”，有三分之一的非洲裔美国人生活在“严重隔离”中，巴尔的摩、费城、纽约等城市是美国种族隔离最严重的城市。

29日　皮尤中心发布的报告显示，大多数美国人反对政府大规模收集公民的信息数据。在了解政府监听项目的受访者中，61%的人越来越不相信这是用来服务公共利益的。

六月

1日　美国人口普查局的调查显示，截至2015年6月，美国约有1740万儿童由单亲妈妈抚养，其中45%生活在贫困线以下。

2日　英国《卫报》网站报道，美国中央情报局使用了比去年参议院报告所披露的更为广泛的性虐待以及其他形式的虐待。曾被关押在关塔那摩监狱的囚犯马吉德·可汗说，审讯官将冰水倒在他的生殖器上，对其裸体进行录像，使用金属靴铐嵌束腿脚致其难以动弹，将他裸体悬挂在木梁上长达3天，只提供少量饮用水而没有任何食物——他所遭受的这些酷刑都没有被写入参议院去年发布的中情局虐囚报告。

10日　国际工会联盟发布一份报告，将美国列为系统性地侵犯工人权利的国家之一。

同日，美国有线电视新闻网财经频道网站报道，得克萨斯州麦金利警察局的白人警察暴力对待一名14岁非洲裔女孩的视频在网上广泛传播。现场拍摄视频的白人目击者认为，该警察的行为毫无疑问是出于种族主义动机。

11日　皮尤中心发布的调查报告显示，混合族裔儿童在美国遭受歧视。有55%的混合族裔表示他们听到过关于种族歧视的语言或者被开过类似的玩笑。

15日　《华盛顿邮报》网站报道，22岁的非洲裔男子克里斯·杰克逊在加利福尼亚州南太浩湖一个汽车旅馆试图从窗户爬出时被警察射杀。

17日　美国哥伦比亚广播公司网站报道，21岁的白人男子戴伦·鲁夫当晚在南卡罗莱纳州查尔斯顿一个传统的非洲裔教堂内枪杀了包括牧师在内的9人。

18日　《今日美国》网站报道，盖洛普调查的结果显示，手无寸铁的非洲裔美国人迈克尔·布朗在弗格森被执法人员杀害之后，认为种族关系是国家面临的最重要问题的美国民众大幅增加。68%的非洲裔美国人认为美国刑事司法系统存在种族偏见。

24日　《美国新闻与世界报道》网站报道，美国的教育支出在政府总体支出中所占的比例近五年持续下降，从2011年占比1.27%下降到2015年的1%，总体下降了19.8%。

同日，英国《独立报》报道，美国先后对三位法国总统和其他政府高官进行了长期的电话监听，对此法国政府发言人表示“无法接受”。

25日　《华盛顿邮报》网站报道，41岁的非洲裔男子斯宾塞·麦凯恩在马里兰州奥因斯米尔斯被警察射杀。

七月

2日　《华盛顿邮报》网站报道，23岁的非洲裔男子维克托·伊曼纽尔·拉罗萨在佛罗里达州杰克逊维尔一个院子里被警察射杀。

7日　《华盛顿邮报》网站报道，由美国所主导的联军应对162名叙利亚平民的死亡负责，其中包括51名儿童和35名妇女。

10日　《今日美国》网站报道，美国一些顶尖心理学家帮助美国中央情报局及国防部虐待囚犯。美国心理学家协会的两位前主席成了美国中央情报局专家顾问团的成员，领导该协会道德监督办公室的史蒂芬·本克也瞒着协会获得了一份旨在培训五角大楼审讯官的合同。

12日　英国广播公司网站报道，据维基解密网站披露，美国一直监听日本的内阁官员、银行和公司，监听至少可追溯到8年以前。通过监听，美国获悉了日本在许多问题上的内部讨论，包括贸易对话、气候变化政策、核能和能源政策等，还包括在日本首相官邸召开的秘密会议的内容。美国也一直在监听德国、法国、巴西等国家。

14日　皮尤中心的调查显示，美国贫困儿童占贫困总人口的比例要大于儿童占总人口的比例。18岁以下人口占总人口的四分之一，但18岁以下的贫困人口却占贫困总人口的三分之一。非洲裔和拉美裔的贫困儿童比例更是大大高于其所占人口的比例。

17日　《华盛顿邮报》网站报道，美国民权组织对北卡罗莱纳州通过法律限制提前投票日期、终止同日注册和禁止非选区选民投票提出指控，认为这严重损害了非洲裔美国选民的选举权。

19日　《华盛顿邮报》网站报道，43岁的非洲裔男子塞缪尔·杜波斯在俄亥俄州奥本山被警察射杀。

28日　《赫芬顿邮报》网站报道，美国前总统吉米·卡特接受采访时表示："现在美国只有寡头政治，无限制的政治贿赂成为提名总统候选人或当选总统的主要影响因素。州长、参议员和国会成员的情况也是如此。美国的政治体系已经被颠覆为向主要政治捐助者提供回报的工具。"普通美国人的意愿微不足道，对公共政策的影响接近于零。

31日　《金融时报》网站报道，美国法律允许超级政治行动委员会从个人和企业筹集不受限额的资金，这改变了美国的政治格局，使亿万和百万富翁们可以更高效地向竞选者提供巨额的资金支持。美国一些最富有的家族希望花钱来影响选举结果。向2016年总统候选人提供百万美元以上捐款者的数量预计将大大超过此前历届选举。

同日，《今日美国》网站报道，根据全美地产经纪商协会3月份的报告，房租和家庭收入之间的差距已经扩大到无法维持的水平。

同日，联合国关于买卖儿童、儿童卖淫和儿童色情制品问题特别报告员莫德·布尔·布基契奥向联合国提交报告指出，同性恋者、跨性别者和双性者在美国的离家出走、无家可归青年救助方案和儿童福利体系中所占比例极大，他们中有42%的人受过性剥削。

八月

3日　在联合国秘书长向第70届联大提交的《有效促进〈在民族或族裔、宗教和语言上属于少数群体者权利宣言〉》的文件中，联合国人权委员会对美国仍对种族定性的做法以及执法人员对某些族裔群体特别是穆斯林的监视继续予以关切。联合国特别报告员等曾在2014年12月对美国裁定米歇尔·布朗案和埃里克·加纳案不予审判表示关切。

4日　《美国新闻与世界报道》网站报道，2010年以来，已经有21个州通过了新的法律来限制投票权的行使，一些州缩短了提前投票时间，其他的州则限制了证明合法选民身份的有效文件的数量。有14个州将在2016年的总统大选中首次实施限制投票权行使的新措施。公民选举权成为两党恶性竞争的牺牲品。

同日，美国全国广播公司财经频道网站报道，2015年受托人社会保障和医疗保险的信托基金报告显示，美国社会保障系统已有25.8万亿美元的亏损。

同日，在联合国秘书长提交给第70届联大的《在反恐中保护人权和基本自由》的文件中，联合国人权事务委员会在审查美国的情况时指出，警察或安全部队成员在逮捕、审讯恐怖主义嫌犯时有计划地实施酷刑、虐待行为或过度使用武力。委员会特别指出没有看到美国关闭关塔那摩监狱的时间表，呼吁美国尽快移交指定要移交的被羁押者。

5日　皮尤中心的调查显示，有53%的白人认为美国当前需要加强种族平等，比2014年高出14个百分点。86%的非洲裔美国人认为必须继续作出改变来实现种族平等。

7日　联合国酷刑问题特别报告员胡安·门德斯向联合国提交的报告中指出，美国中情局在2001年9月11日后实施特别引渡和秘密拘留方案，与其他国家相互协作和协助对个人实施绑架、转移、法外拘押和酷刑。

12日　联合国秘书长向第70届联大提交的《关于儿童权利公约的现状》的报告指出，美国仍未批准或加入《儿童权利公约》。美国是目前唯一一个没有批准或加入《儿童权利公约》的国家。

15日　《今日美国》网站报道，数据显示，47%的农村拉美裔婴儿出生于贫困家庭。康奈尔大学的研究人员指出："这些孩子一出生就输在了人生的起跑线上，面临不能健康成长的风险。"

18日　皮尤中心报告显示，美国社会保障2015年的收支差距预计大约是840亿美元。据预测，社会保障综合储备到2034年可能完全枯竭。残疾人保险信托基金可能在2016年底就会枯竭，养老和抚恤金预计在2035年被耗尽。

23日　博根项目网站报道，美国医疗护理水平在11个发达国家中排倒数第一，婴儿死亡率最高，在预防死亡方面排名倒数第二。

24日　美国广播公司网站报道，最新调查显示，美国正在接受治疗的吸毒者中五分之一的人是在18岁之前通过父母初次接触毒品的，其中6%的人甚至使用过海洛因。

26日　美国哥伦比亚广播公司弗吉尼亚州分支机构电视台的一名记者和一名摄影师当日早晨现场直播采访时被枪击身亡。凶手发给美国广播公司传真表示，他的作案动机源于2015年6月一名白人在南卡罗莱纳州非洲裔教堂实施的枪击案。

九月

1日　美国联邦调查局发布《2014年美国犯罪报告》。2014年美国共发生1165383起暴力犯罪，其中严重暴力伤害案件占暴力犯罪案件的63.6%，抢劫案件占28%，强奸案件占7.2%，谋杀案件占1.2%。在67.9%的谋杀案件、40.3%的抢劫案件和22.5%的严重暴力犯罪案件中使用了枪支。2014年美国共发生8277829起财产犯罪案件。被害人因财产犯罪（排除纵火犯罪）而遭受的损失达到143亿美元。

9日　《今日美国》网站报道，由全美律师协会及非洲裔律师和法官发布的民意调查显示，88%的非洲裔和59%的白人认为非洲裔美国人受到了警察的不公平待遇。

10日 英国《每日邮报》网站报道，美国政府阻止公开美国中央情报局在关塔那摩监狱虐待基地组织成员细节的文件。现年44岁的阿布·祖巴耶达赫于2002年被捕，自2006年便被关押在关塔那摩监狱。他曾在一个月中遭受83次水刑并失去一目。他的辩护律师透露已经提交了一份长达116页的祖巴耶达赫受虐口述，并指控中央情报局曾要求祖巴耶达赫不得披露受虐的细节。

16日 《今日美国》网站报道，一名微软公司前员工向法院起诉微软公司歧视女性，指控微软公司"全面侵犯女性技术员工的权利，并导致在其企业文化中泛滥着性别偏见"。这一诉讼正在演化为集体诉讼。

18日 政策创新研究所网站发表文章指出，尽管美国现任总统曾许诺在他第一个任期结束时签署全民医保法案，但到2014年，美国仍然有3300万人没有医疗保险。

21日 《洛杉矶时报》《华盛顿邮报》网站报道，美国高等院校联合会发布的一项针对美国27所大学15万学生的网上调查显示，超过四分之一的女大学生表示自己曾是性侵害的受害者。在南加利福尼亚州大学，29.7%的大学本科女生报告称受到过严重的性侵，在全国各大学校园中遭受严重性侵的大学本科女生的比例为13%至30%。

22日 《华盛顿邮报》发表文章指出，在美国不信仰基督教的人想竞选公职很困难，不信仰任何宗教的人想竞选公职则更加困难。皮尤中心的调查显示，在所有与宗教相关的群体中，美国人对无神论者和穆斯林群体的看法最为负面。

23日 《华盛顿邮报》网站报道，19岁的非洲裔男子基思·哈里森·麦克劳德在马里兰州一个药房内被发现试图伪造处方，警察在追逐中将其射杀。

十月

1日 英国《卫报》网站发表《美国何时将修复其残破的民主》一文称，观察当今的美国政治就是观看金钱的角逐。2016年的美国大选几乎肯定会成为史上最昂贵的选举。

2日 《芝加哥论坛报》《赫芬顿邮报》网站报道，俄勒冈州罗森伯格市乌姆普夸社区学院的学生克里斯·莫瑟尔10月1日身穿防弹衣、携带6支枪闯入该学院一间教室，开枪打死9人、打伤9人后自杀。这是2015年美国第45起校园枪击事件。自2012年12月4日桑迪胡克小学枪击案以来，美国已经发生了142起校园枪击事件。

3日 美国有线电视新闻网、俄罗斯新闻网网站报道，阿富汗昆都士的“无国界医生”组织医院10月3日受到美军空袭，造成42人遇难，其中包括12名医疗工作人员和3名儿童。“无国界医生”组织指控美军的空袭是“战争罪行”而非“人为失误”。

5日 《华盛顿邮报》网站报道，27岁的奥马尔·阿里在俄亥俄州阿克伦城一个酒吧内被警察开枪打死。

8日 卡塔尔半岛电视台美国频道网站报道，根据美国农业部的最新数据，美国大约五分之一的儿童生活在食品保障不足的家庭。2014年美国有15.4%的人口生活在粮食保障不足的家庭，总计超过4800万人。

10日 《今日美国》网站报道，美国的贫富差距在20世纪80年代大幅拉大并持续恶化，低收入美国人想要向上流动越来越困难。美国最穷的20%人口的收入仅占总收入的3.1%，而最富的20%人口的收入却占总收入的51.4%。据统计，美国一半以上的财富属于最富的3%的人口。

同日，英国广播公司、俄罗斯电视台网站报道，美国北亚利桑那大学和得克萨斯南方大学10月9日分别发生一起大学校园枪击案，使美国2015年的校园枪击案攀升到52起，其中30人被杀，53人受伤。

14日 法新社报道，10月14日公布的统计数据表明，纽约是一个极度不平等的城市，十分贫穷的布鲁克林区的居民要比生活在华尔街附近的富裕居民平均少活11年。

15日 英国《每日邮报》网站报道，被曝光的有关美国无人机暗杀计划的绝密细节显示，90%被杀死的人都不是预先要攻击的目标。2012年1月至2013年2月在阿富汗东北部所发动的一场代号为“干草机”的行动中，大约有219人被炸死，但仅有35人是预先要攻击的目标，命中准确率只有15%，并且所有的死者都被贴上“阵亡敌人”的标签。

22日 美国在线网站报道，美国许多大城市当日举行针对警察暴行的抗议活动。抗议活动组织者在网站上列出了美国警察暴行的五大惊人特征：（1）2015年有920多人被警察杀死；（2）在没带武器的情况下，非洲裔美国人遭遇警察时被杀的概率是白人的两倍；（3）美国土著人被执法人员杀害的概率与非洲裔一样高；（4）过度使用暴力是警察不当行为中最为常见的一种形式；（5）警察杀死1000个人，才会有1名警察被判有罪。

23日 美国哥伦比亚巡回法院上诉法庭当日作出判决，裁定一名在国外对美国公民阿米尔·马歇尔实施非法拘禁、审讯和酷刑长达4个月的联邦探员将不会被问责。马歇尔在辗转多个国家的监狱，遭受单独囚禁和酷刑、死亡威胁被送回美国后，体重减少了80磅。但哥伦比亚巡回法院上诉法庭却裁决他不能因这种侵权行为而起诉联邦政府。

同日，《基督教科学箴言报》网站报道，美国商会是美国最大的商业游说团体，它计划在2016年选举中发挥“积极”作用。该商会称，相对于2014年选举中花费的7000万美元，对2016年选举的付出将增加到1亿美元。

31日 据美国无家可归者联盟统计，纽约市无家可归者人数已达到自20世纪30年代“大萧条”以来的最高水平。2015年10月纽约共有59568名无家可归者每天晚上是在庇护场所里度过的，其中包括14361个无家可归的家庭和23858名无家可归的儿童。目前，每天在纽约市庇护所过夜的无家可归者人数比10年前高出86%。每天晚上还有成千上万衣衫褴褛的无家可归者露宿在纽约街头、地铁和其他公共空间或场所里。

十一月

3日 《华盛顿邮报》网站报道，6岁的杰里米·马蒂斯在拉斯维加斯马克斯维尔被警察开枪打死。

同日，美国经济政策研究所发布的第三季度失业数据调查显示，非洲裔美国人的失业率长期是白人的大约2倍。差距最大的是哥伦比亚特区，其非洲裔失业率比白人高出5.7倍。

10日 《今日美国》网站报道，美国快餐店工人当日同时在数百个城市罢工并上街示威游行，要求每小时15美元的最低工资。

11日 美国有线电视新闻网报道，一位共和党总统竞选人被问到如何将1100万非法移民从美国消除时，说他将组建一只“驱逐部队”以消除1100万移民，他还主张取消公民因出生在美国而具有美国国籍的公民权利。

同日，皮尤慈善信托组织网站报道，自9月以来，洛杉矶、西雅图、俄勒冈州的波特兰以及夏威夷州先后宣布紧急状态来缓解日益恶化的无家可归危机。洛杉矶约有25000名无家可归者。

12日 《华盛顿邮报》网站报道，美国疾病控制和防治中心11月12日发布的报告显示,美国新生儿患有梅毒的比率2012年至2014年增长了38%。2014年每100000个出生的婴儿中有11.6例患有梅毒。

15日 美国有线电视新闻网报道，非洲裔美国人贾马尔·克拉克当日凌晨被警察射杀。目击者称克拉克当时已被戴上手铐，一名警察将膝盖顶在他的背上，另一名警察则骑着他使他动弹不得，没有看到他反抗。

16日 美国联邦调查局发布《2014年仇恨犯罪统计》，2014年共发生仇恨犯罪事件5479件和仇恨违法案件6418件。在5462件单一偏见犯罪事件中涉及6681名受害者，其中48.3%的受害者受到攻击是由于犯罪者的种族偏见，17.1%的受害者受到攻击是由于犯罪者的宗教信仰偏见。

17日 《华盛顿邮报》网站报道，截至2015年11月17日上午，美国27个州长都表示反对让来自叙利亚的难民安置在他们的州。一些共和党议员和总统候选人甚至呼吁出台禁止叙利亚穆斯林难民进入美国的禁令。

同日，美国公共宗教研究所发布的调查结果显示，63%的被调查者认为非洲裔在美国面临很大的歧视，56%的被调查者认为拉美裔在美国面临很大的歧视，70%的被调查者认为美国存在许多对穆斯林的歧视，45%的被调查者认为美国存在许多对妇女的歧视。

18日　《美国新闻与世界报道》网站报道，研究人员发现，18%的学生在进入大学校园之前在丧失行动能力的情况下被强奸过，其中41%的年轻女学生在大学一年级期间在丧失行动能力情况下被再次强奸过。美国疾病控制和防治中心的数据显示，五分之一的女性曾被强奸，其中很大一部分是被熟人强奸。

19日　《今日美国》网站报道，约2000名机场工作人员从11月18日晚到19日在美国7个主要机场进行罢工，以抗议过低的工资水平，要求每小时15美元的最低工资。

同日，英国《卫报》网站报道，一位共和党美国总统候选人接受采访时表示，不排除利用数据库跟踪美国的穆斯林，或发给他们标注了其宗教信仰的特殊身份证件。他还表示将考虑对穆斯林进行无证搜查，并增加对清真寺的监控。

23日　《芝加哥论坛报》报道，美国移民法院处理案件效率低下。芝加哥移民法院目前积压案件已达1.7万件，有关案件普遍已经候审长达2年半，一些案件要到2020年才能开始听证。在这些案件中，大约600件是儿童移民案，久拖不决给当事儿童及其家庭带来巨大痛苦。

24日　美国有线电视新闻网报道，被控射杀17岁非洲裔男孩麦克唐纳的芝加哥警察曾遭受20项投诉，却从来没有受到过处分。人们对2014年10月枪杀事件发生以来13个月才起诉该警官表示愤怒，在芝加哥市的大街上举行示威抗议，要求为麦克唐纳之死伸张正义。

26日　英国《卫报》网站报道，政府数据显示，2008年至2014年，美国每年至少有4810万人均衡饮食无法得到保障，其中包括19.2%有孩子的家庭。

30日　《华盛顿邮报》网站报道，当日公布的一份文件披露的所谓“国家安全密函”的细节显示，美国联邦调查局强迫互联网公司向其提供用户信息，包括全部的网络浏览历史。联邦调查局利用这种密函来进行电子监控而无须经过法庭批准。

十二月

1日　英国《卫报》网站报道，自2002年以来，现年37岁的穆斯塔法·阿齐兹·沙米里便在未经审判的情况下被美国无限期关押在关塔那摩监狱，长达13年。

2日　《今日美国》网站报道，两名枪手当日冲进位于圣贝纳迪诺的一所社会服务机构，向参加一个假日聚会的人们开火，造成14人死亡和17人受伤。

10日　皮尤中心发布最新研究报告指出，由于收入增长缓慢或停滞，美国的中产阶级逐渐萎缩，在总人口中所占比例由1971年的61%下降到目前的49.9%。这是美国中产阶级人口比例首次低于50%。

11日　《今日美国》网站报道，俄克拉荷马州前警官丹尼尔·霍尔茨克劳被认定在自己巡逻的一个低收入社区性侵女性。他被判与8名受害女性有关的18项罪名，其中有4项一级强奸罪，这8名女性都是非洲裔。调查显示，在6年的时间里约1000名警官由于性犯罪或其他不正当的性行为而失去警官执业资格。

同日，联合国在法律和实践中歧视妇女问题专家组结束对美国为期10天的访问时指出，美国政府在2010年和2015年两次接受联合国人权理事会普遍定期审议时均承诺批准《消除对妇女一切形式歧视公约》，但这一承诺至今尚未兑现。美国在保障妇女权利方面落后于国际人权标准。

12日　英国广播公司网站报道，对美国5个城市的研究显示，人们在申请住房时会因其姓名而受到歧视。名字听起来像非洲裔美国人的申请者申请住房时得到的回应比名字听起来像白人的申请者少16%。

13日　《迈阿密先驱报》网站报道，美国最大的女子监狱罗维尔监狱充斥着腐败及性丑闻。女囚们投诉称，2011年到2015年5月，针对她们的性侵在浴室、壁橱、洗衣室和狱警办公室均有发生。

15日　《基督教科学箴言报》网站报道，美国总统在2007年便承诺要关闭关塔那摩监狱，但直到2015年12月15日，该监狱仍有107名在押嫌疑人。联合国指出，在不经公诉和审判的前提下无限期关押嫌疑人违反国际法，呼吁美国关闭这所监狱。

16日　《迈阿密先驱报》网站发表文章，披露了狱警帕特里克·奎尔西奥里在罗维尔女子监狱中的腐败和暴行。虽然奎尔西奥里曾被逮捕过两次，但佛罗里达监狱系统2004年仍然雇佣了他。他被囚犯们称为罗维尔监狱中最危险的狱警之一。在过去10年中，已经有57名囚犯死在了罗维尔监狱，这个数字并不包括被送往医院的囚犯。

同日，《华尔街日报》与美国全国广播公司联合调查显示，美国的种族关系正处于20年来最糟的时期。2015年12月，只有34%的美国人认为种族关系足够好或非常好，比2009年下降了43个百分点。

同日，“空中战争跟踪组织”网站报道，2014年8月8日至2015年12月16日，伊拉克和叙利亚有757名至1073名平民在123件空袭事件中被美国主导的联军杀害。

17日　美国“拦截”网站报道，美国情报机构使用技术手段长期大规模监听普通民众。“黄貂鱼”“垃圾盒”等一系列程序都可以被美国国家安全局或中央情报局用于监听手机和短信，甚至可以提取手机内媒体文件、地址簿及被删除的短信。

18日　美国疾病控制和防治中心发布的报告显示，美国因药物服用过量（主要是止痛药和海洛因）致死人数再创新高。2014年超过47000人死于药物服用过量，比2013年增加了约6%。

24日　俄罗斯卫星新闻网报道，美国国防部前雇员、导弹技术专家西奥多·波斯托尔接受采访时表示，平民至今仍是美国核力量的潜在打击目标。他说：“事实是，平民从一开始，并且至今都是我们的目标。”

27日　《华盛顿邮报》网站报道，一名芝加哥警察12月26日在处置一场家庭纠纷报警时反应过度，射杀了19岁的勒格利尔及其55岁的邻居贝蒂·琼斯。

28日　美国枪支暴力档案室网站发布《2015年枪支暴力伤亡统

计》，2015年美国共发生枪支暴力事件51675起，其中大规模枪击事件329起；共造成13136人死亡、26493人受伤，其中0岁至11岁的儿童伤亡682人，12岁至17岁的少年伤亡2640人。

31日 据《华盛顿邮报》网站统计，美国警察2015年共射杀990人。按照月份统计，美国警察2015年1月射杀76人，2月射杀77人，3月射杀92人，4月射杀84人，5月射杀71人，6月射杀65人，7月射杀104人，8月射杀94人，9月射杀80人，10月射杀82人，11月射杀76人，12月射杀89人。